PORTSMOUTH PO

CONSUMER POLICY

IN OECD COUNTRIES

1983

ORGANISATION FOR ECONOMIC CO-OPERATION AND DEVELOPMENT

Pursuant to article 1 of the Convention signed in Paris on 14th December, 1960, and which came into force on 30th September, 1961, the Organisation for Economic Co-operation and Development (OECD) shall promote policies designed:

- to achieve the highest sustainable economic growth and employment and a rising standard of living in Member countries, while maintaining financial stability, and thus to contribute to the development of the world economy;
- to contribute to sound economic expansion in Member as well as non-member countries in the process of economic development; and
- to contribute to the expansion of world trade on a multilateral, non-discriminatory basis in accordance with international obligations.

The Signatories of the Convention on the OECD are Austria, Belgium, Canada, Denmark, France, the Federal Republic of Germany, Greece, Iceland, Ireland, Italy, Luxembourg, the Netherlands, Norway, Portugal, Spain, Sweden, Switzerland, Turkey, the United Kingdom and the United States. The following countries acceded subsequently to this Convention (the dates are those on which the instruments of accession were deposited): Japan (28th April, 1964), Finland (28th January, 1969), Australia (7th June, 1971) and New Zealand (29th May, 1973).

The Socialist Federal Republic of Yugoslavia takes part in certain work of the OECD (agreement of 28th October, 1961).

Publié en français sous le titre:

**LA POLITIQUE
A L'ÉGARD DES CONSOMMATEURS
DANS LES PAYS DE L'OCDE**
1983

The OECD Committee on Consumer Policy regularly reviews developments in the field of consumer policy on the basis of annual reports submitted by Member countries.

The present reports, which were submitted to the Committee at its meeting in June 1984, cover the calendar year 1983 and concern 21 Member countries: Australia, Austria, Belgium, Canada, Denmark, Finland, France, Germany, Greece, Ireland, Japan, Luxembourg, the Netherlands, New Zealand, Norway, Portugal, Spain, Sweden, Switzerland, the United Kingdom, the United States and the Commission of the European Communities. They describe institutional developments, new enactments and amendments to existing regulations aimed at protecting the safety and the economic interest of consumers, as well as measures of consumer information and education. The reports are preceded by a summary describing the main developments and highlighting new trends in policy and legislation.

Also available

PRODUCT SAFETY. Measures to Protect Children (July 1984)
(24 84 03 1) ISBN 92-64-12588-4   86 pages   £4.50   US$9.00   F45.00

PRODUCT SAFETY – RISK MANAGEMENT AND COST-BENEFIT ANALYSIS.
"Document" Series (December 1983)
(24 83 02 1)ISBN 92-64-12510-8   106 pages   £5.00   US$10.00   F50.00

CONSUMER POLICY DURING THE PAST TEN YEARS – MAIN DEVELOP-MENTS AND PROSPECTS (November 1983)
(24 83 04 1) ISBN 92-64-12521-3   88 pages   £4.50   US$9.00   F45.00

COMPUTER TECHNOLOGIES AND CONSUMER INFORMATION. Interactive
Videotex Systems. "Document" Series (February 1983)
(24 82 05 1) ISBN 92-64-12389-X   36 pages   £3.30   US$6.50   F33.00

ADVERTISING DIRECTED AT CHILDREN – ENDORSEMENT IN ADVERTIS-ING. "Document" Series (July 1982)
(24 82 02 1) ISBN 92-64-12276-1   64 pages   £2.70   US$6.00   F27.00

RECALL PROCEDURES FOR UNSAFE PRODUCTS SOLD TO THE PUBLIC.
"Document" Series (October 1981)
(24 81 05 1) ISBN 92-64-12248-6   64 pages   £3.00   US$6.75   F30.00

**SAFETY OF CONSUMER PRODUCTS – Policy and Legislation in OECD Member
Countries. "Document" Series (June 1981)**
(24 80 05 1) ISBN 92-64-12130-7   88 pages   £3.20   US$8.00   F32.00

CONSUMER PROTECTION CONCERNING AIR PACKAGE TOURS. "Document"
Series (July 1980)
(24 80 02 1) ISBN 92-64-12077-7   44 pages   £2.00   US$4.50   F18.00

BARGAIN PRICE OFFERS AND SIMILAR MARKETING PRACTICES. "Document"
Series (May 1980)
(24 80 01 1) ISBN 92-64-12033-5   56 pages   £2.70   US$6.00   F23.00

**MAIL ORDER TRADING AND OTHER SELECTED DISTANT SELLING
METHODS. "Document" Series (November 1978)**
(24 78 05 1) ISBN 92-64-11858-6   52 pages   £2.50   US$5.00   F20.00

Prices charged at the OECD Publications Office.

*THE OECD CATALOGUE OF PUBLICATIONS and supplements will be sent free of charge
on request addressed either to OECD Publications Office,
2, rue André-Pascal, 75775 PARIS CEDEX 16, or to the OECD Sales Agent in your country.*

TABLE OF CONTENTS

Main developments in the field of consumer policy 7

ANNUAL REPORTS

5

MAIN DEVELOPMENTS IN THE FIELD OF CONSUMER POLICY

I. INTRODUCTION

1.   During the past decade the majority of Member countries have developed an institutional and legal framework for handling consumer concerns. The 1983 reports submitted by Member countries show that this machinery had to deal with a very large variety of consumer problems: some have been lingering on for years -- consumer credit and various marketing problems, e.g. with second-hand cars, would be prominent examples in this context; new problems are emerging with the technological changes in distribution and banking and there is also a growing consumer policy involvement with questions arising in connection with wider socio-economic concerns such as environmental problems, deregulation and the strengthening of competition.

2.   The following review traces the main developments in the consumer policy field, referring in particular to important new measures, questions which occupy simultaneously a number of countries, and issues that have been raised in the above-mentioned broader context of economic policies.

II. INSTITUTIONAL DEVELOPMENTS

3.   One of the probably most important institutional events took place at the level of the European Communities. The first ever Council of Ministers responsible for Consumer Affairs was held on 12th December 1983 in Brussels. It was followed by two other Consumer Affairs Councils in 1984, and brought new impetus to the implementation of the Communities' consumer programme.

4.   The majority of institutional developments notified by Member countries concerned transformations and re-organisations of mainly technical nature. In Australia, for instance, where consumer policy had recently been transferred to the Attorney-General, it has now been taken over by the Minister for Home Affairs and Environment. In Austria, a reorganiation of ministerial responsibilities has led to the creation of a new Ministry for Family, Youth and Consumer Affairs, which is in charge of the consumer policy activities -- both physical and economic protection -- formerly dealt with by the Ministry for Trade and Industry. In France, where the former Ministry for Consumer Affairs had been transformed into a State Secretariat in the Ministry of Economic Affairs, Finance and the Budget, responsible for Consumer Affairs, the National Consumer Affairs Committee has, in the course of this reform, become a

National Consumer Affairs Council which comprises representatives of consumer and user groups and the business community. In the United Kingdom, the Department of Trade and the Department of Industry have been merged and consumer policy is now being dealt with in a Consumer and Corporate Affairs Unit in the Department of Trade and Industry.

5.   Considerable progress has been made with regard to the representation of consumer views in some Member countries. In Australia, for example, a new Economic Planning Advisory Council has been established as a follow-up to a National Economic Summit Conference and is intended to continue the process of co-operation and consultation between Commonwealth and state governments, industry, unions and community groups begun at the Conference. It has a representative of the Australian Federation of Consumer Organisation as one of the inaugural members. In Portugal, a 1983 Decree-Law now clearly determines the consumer protection responsibilities of the newly created Ministry for the Quality of Life, which is mandated not only to study, promote and participate in consumer protection policy, but also to collaborate in the formulation and approval of regulations reflecting the consumer protection standpoint. An Office of Consumer Protection which has been created within the Ministry, is to provide the technical basis for this work together with the National Consumer Institute. Moreover, consumers are well represented in a number of newly created commissions and advisory boards. In Spain, two important changes were the creation of a Health and Consumer Action Unit, which is in charge of taking immediate action in a risk situation and to co-ordinate resources, and the establishment of an Interministerial Commission to co-ordinate inspection services for durable consumer goods and services, which is chaired by the Secretary-General for Consumer Affairs; his principal role is to co-ordinate the inspection activities of various other ministries and provincial and municipal authorities.

6.   The decentralisation of consumer information and advice bodies is being continued in the Nordic countries. Four new consumer advice centres have been created in Finland, where such centres now cover 58 per cent of the total population and in Norway, the systematic decentralisation of the Consumer Council by according supplementary resources directly to the local offices has been pursued in 1983. In Sweden, consumer advice centres now exist in 207 of the 284 municipalities, thus being available to about 90 per cent of the population.

III. PRODUCT SAFETY

7.   The product safety sector increasingly demonstrates the international aspects of consumer policy both with regard to hazard reaction activities taken in connection with internationally traded goods and with regard to the handling of safety problems of general character. The national development reports reflect the effect of the informal notification procedure operated within the Committee on consumer policy in connection with new regulations, product laws and recalls and safety research. The incoming notifications are effectively used in monitoring the marketplace and frequently appropriate action immediately follows the notification of product safety problems in other countries.

8

8.   In addition, certain safety concerns occupy the consumer policy authorities of various Member countries at the same time. The utilisation of urea formaldehyde in insulation is a case in point. <u>Canada, Denmark, the United Kingdom and the United States</u> report research work and/or extensive discussion concerning the possible health hazards connected with the utilisation of this material in housing.

9.   Moreover, the country reports show increased research activities in the field of product safety in general and also present some preliminary results of data collection systems recording product-related accidents. In the <u>Netherlands</u>, for example, the Consumer Safety Foundation has started the accident registration system in 17 hospitals, and in <u>Sweden</u>, first results of data collection activities have become available, which show that roughly 10 per cent of the population can be expected to be involved in product-related accidents severe enough to merit recording. In the <u>United Kingdom</u>, the Home Accident Surveillance System (HASS) has been used extensively by manufacturers, government departments, research associations and consumer organisations.

10.   During the past years, several Member countries have reshaped their product safety provisions with the introduction of overall consumer product safety laws which provide for a comprehensive scope and flexible mechanisms to tackle safety problems arising in the marketplace. In 1983, Austria and France have introduced such legislation. In <u>Austria</u>, the new Product Safety Act came into force in September 1983. It not only contains a list of protective measures and the instruments for applying them but also provides for the creation of an Advisory Board in charge of preparing expert opinions in connection with specific measures to be taken. In <u>France</u>, the new law of 21st July 1983 on product safety is also based on the above principles -- comprehensiveness and flexibility -- and includes the creation of a special "Product Safety Commission". Moreover, it provides for the possibility of prohibiting the export of hazardous products.

IV. PROTECTION OF THE CONSUMER'S ECONOMIC INTERESTS

11.   Regulatory activities in this field continued in 1983 in Member countries with a certain domination of subjects situated in the service sector. The reorganisation of consumer credit laws which has been going on for several years in Member countries, and still continued in 1983. In <u>Denmark</u>, a new Consumer Credit Act came into force in April. One of its major aims is to improve information on the actual costs of consumer credit. Moreover, the act prohibits the use of mortgages and of bills of exchange in consumer credit transactions. Other bills recently introduced concerned debt reorganisation for heavily indebted consumers, and credit cards. In the <u>Netherlands</u>, a new regulation requires the indication of the effective rate of interest in consumer credit advertisements and contracts. In <u>Japan</u>, two study groups dealing with consumer credit presented their reports in 1983 and the Ministry of International Trade and Industry is currently preparing an amendment to the Credit Sales Act. Laws regulating money-lending business were also introduced and the Economic Planning Agency promoted consumer education concerning lease problems. In <u>Switzerland</u>, the Consumer Credit Act is before Parliament and in the <u>United Kingdom</u>, various regulations were made to implement the remaining provisions of the 1974 Consumer Credit Act, which will come into force in May

9

1985 and include consumers' rights to cancel credit agreements made in the consumer's home and to obtain a rebate for early settlements. In the United States, the Federal Trade Commission has actively enforced consumer credit laws governing such areas as advertising and discrimination on grounds of sex, race, age or other factors.

12.   Another service area which increasingly occupied policy-makers in 1983 was insurance business. In Australia, the Insurance (Agents and Brokers) Act is aimed at regulating the activities of insurance intermediaries with a view to strengthening the financial stability of the industry overall and protecting the public from harmful practices as well as negligence and misconduct by intermediaries. The Insurance Contracts' Act will implement reforms suggested by a Law Reform Commission Report on insurance contracts. The Act is intended to improve the flow of information between the insurer and the insured and to provide a uniform and fair set of rules to govern the relationship between the insurer and the insured. The Acts are expected to be proclaimed early in 1985. In the Netherlands, an expert group on life insurance has prepared a report which is to serve as a basis for a regulatory framework providing more consumer information and protection, and in New Zealand, an Insurance Law Reform Bill was introduced at the end of 1983.

13.   Consumer problems with real estate transactions are another area which have attracted the attention of policy-makers in several Member countries. In Canada, the Government put forward several proposals suggesting improvements in the mortgage market. In Japan, the Ministry of Construction has formed an Examination Committee to improve the complaints settlement procedures in this field and in Sweden, Parliament has passed an Act on Real Estate Agents which includes provisions concerning professional requirements, insurance covering the agent's commitments vis-à-vis sellers and buyers, and fair information requirements.

14.   Other problem areas which continued to occupy consumer authorities were the travel industry, unfair contract terms and the impact of new technologies in banking and distribution.

V. CONSUMER INFORMATION AND EDUCATION

15.   In most countries, consumer information activities directly reflect the consumer concerns of the day. Certain aspects of food labelling for instance seem to have found a broad interest in 1983. The use of terms like "natural" in food labelling and advertising is the subject of industry guidelines currently being developed in Canada. In Germany, all prepacked foodstuff labels must now carry information concerning minimum durability and ingredients. In Spain, the general rules for the labelling, presentation and advertising of foodstuffs came into force in March 1984. In the United States, the Federal Trade Commission pursued many types of deceptive practices, including in particular health and nutrition claims in food and advertising.

16.   While Member countries generally report a continuing effort in promoting consumer information through the now already established channels, e.g. product labelling and publication of comparative tests, and the Netherlands in particular stress the need to strengthen consumer information in the mass

media, it has also to be noted that two countries, Portugal and Spain, which up to now had not yet been strongly involved in such activities, have now started regulating and actively promoting consumer information. In Portugal, consumer organisations have started publishing comparative tests, and in Spain, a Royal Decree sets out rules for carrying out analysis and publicising results via the media. Five comparative tests on foodstuffs and cosmetics have been carried out and released in collaboration with the Spanish Television Authority.

17. On a broader regulatory level, Switzerland reports the preparation of a Consumer Information Bill which will prohibit the supply of certain goods and services unless they are accompanied by specified information. Moreover, amendments to the contract law and the competition law also include reversal of the burden of proof in advertising claims.

18. The inclusion of consumer education at school level continued to be pursued in many Member countries. Several countries, however, also consider that these efforts have not been entirely successful up to now. Norway, for example, points out that, although consumer education has been mandatory for ten years, there still is an evident lack of good teaching aids capable of being usefully integrated into other subjects.

19. On the other hand, some countries have attempted to give consumer education a broader basis which takes into account the need to educate educators and to address appropriate efforts to the business community. In France, for instance, the Université de Haute Alsace offers a special course for the consumer educators. In Australia, a special educational effort has been addressed towards the business community. In particular small business guidance was given priority in the form of meetings and brochures dealing with statutory and voluntary guarantees, recommended prices and problems with franchising.

VI. REDRESS AND COMPLAINTS FACILITIES

20. Many Member countries note a growing interest in mediation and arbitration mechanisms or other simplified procedures. In Belgium, sectoral complaints and arbitration boards have been created in co-operation with the professional groups concerned, in the furniture, travel, real estate and dry cleaning business. In Canada, where the Council of Better Business Bureaux is adding formal mediation and arbitration programmes to its conciliation activities, the Canadian Bar Association has also launched two pilot projects that offer mediation and arbitration services. In the Netherlands, the Ministry of Justice announced its intention to draft a bill aimed at simplifying procedures for minor civil cases, and New Zealand, which in previous reports had already indicated the positive experience gained with Small Claims Tribunals, opened five new courts of this type, bringing their total number to 18. In Switzerland, the Cantons are currently preparing simplified legal procedures provided for in the 1981 constitutional provisions on consumer protection and the United Kingdom reports that the use of small claims courts has continued to increase in 1983.

VII. GENERAL REMARKS

21.   During the past years there has been a growing awareness of the inter-
actions between consumer policy and other policy concerns in the
socio-economic field and the 1983 reports clearly reflect the impact of certain general trends in economic policy on consumer policy on the one hand, and
an increasing interest consumer policy now takes in developments in other
policy areas. The heightened sensitivity to the implicit cost to the private
sector -- and, finally to consumers -- of regulatory initiatives has, for
example, led to a careful evaluation of proposed consumer laws and to a
stronger reliance on industry-wide self regulation. On the other hand, consumer representatives have also requested and enhanced deregulation in sectors
where protectionist arrangements have impeded competition both at national or
international level. A large number of reports therefore directly or indirectly refer to the role consumer policy could play in the development of
competition and free trade in the interest of consumers and the economy as a
whole.

AUSTRALIA

Part I of this report covers developments at the national (i.e. Commonwealth Government) level for the 1983 calendar year and Part II covers developments at the State and Territorial levels for the same period.

Part I

COMMONWEALTH GOVERNMENT

I. INSTITUTIONAL DEVELOPMENTS IN THE FIELD OF CONSUMER POLICY

1.   Following the change of Government in March 1983, responsibility for the consumer protection provisions of the Trade Practices Act was transferred from the Attorney-General to the Minister for Home Affairs and Environment. This transfer of Ministerial responsibility did not involve any change in the responsibility of the Commonwealth Government for consumer affairs.

2.   On 15th June 1983, a meeting of Commonwealth, State, and Territory Consumer Affairs Ministers in Canberra discussed uniformity of consumer protection laws and, in particular, the possibility of State Governments introducing legislation to mirror the consumer protection provisions of the Trade Practices Act.

3.   Commonwealth budget allocations for consumer affairs activities are made to the Department of Home Affairs and Environment and to the Trade Practices Commission (TPC). These allocations are for the total responsibilities of these organisations and it would not be possible to easily isolate the amounts allocated for consumer affairs activities. The Commonwealth Government provides an annual grant to the Australian Federation of Consumer Organisations which for the 1983-84 financial year was increased to $120 000 from $100 000 in 1982-83.

4.   A National Economic Summit Conference was held in April 1983 to provide a forum for the expression of views and to encourage consensus on issues important to the future of Australia. The participants in the Conference were broadly representative of Australian political, economic and social interests. It was agreed at the Conference that an Economic Planning Advisory Council (EPAC) should be established to continue the process of co-operation

and consultation begun at the Conference. EPAC came into effect on 8th July 1983. Through EPAC the Government has available to it, on a continuing basis, independent advice from State Governments, industry, unions and community groups which will be utilised in the process of economic-policy formulation. Dr. John Braithwaite, a member of the executive of the Australian Federation of Consumer Organisations (AFCO), was appointed as one of the seventeen inaugural members of EPAC to represent consumers and community groups.

5.   Following the National Economic Summit Conference a Working Party was established to provide advice to the Government on the legislation of the establishment of a prices surveillance body. The Working Party comprised representatives of the trade union movement, business, State and Local Government and community groups, and included Dr. Braithwaite of AFCO. The Working Party was extensively consulted by the Government in drafting the Bill which established the Prices Surveillance Authority (PSA). The PSA, which commenced operations in March 1984, monitors and examines prices, but does not attempt to hold prices down by administrative fiat.

II. REGULATORY OR OTHER ACTION CONCERNING CONSUMER PROTECTION INFORMATION AND EDUCATION, AND MEANS OF REDRESS

1. Consumer Protection

6.   In November 1983 the Minister for Home Affairs and Environment announced the Government's intention to release draft legislation containing extensive and major reforms to the consumer protection provisions (Part V) and related provisions of the Trade Practices Act 1974. (Draft legislation was released for public comment in February 1984.) He said that the proposed amendments were intended to restore and enhance the previously understood operation of the Act, and to improve the Act's ability to protect consumers and reputable business interests.

7.   Some of the more significant proposals related to:

-- A prohibition against unconscionable conduct;

-- The definition of consumer;

-- TPC action on behalf of consumers;

-- Employer's responsibility for their employees;

-- Export of hazardous goods;

-- Time limits for prosecution;

-- Enforcement of payment of fines;

-- Misleading conduct in relation to employment.

8.   The TPC commenced 11 prosecutions during the year. These were related to the protection of consumers' physical and economic interests and included cases dealing with:

-- Misrepresentations that certain bicycles had the approval of the Standards Association of Australia;

-- Supply of children's night garments which failed to comply with mandatory safety standards for flammability; and

-- Fraudulent business franchising schemes.

a) Physical protection (product safety)

9.   Safety standards for children's toys and babies' dummies were further considered throughout the year. In relation to toys the Commonwealth/State Consumer Products Advisory Committee (CSCPAC) decided that the toy industry should be encouraged to comply with voluntary safety standard, Australian Standard 1647 Parts 1, 2, 3 and 4. CSCPAC will monitor the effectiveness of this voluntary standard during 1984.

10.   During the year all babies' dummies available on the Australian market were tested for compliance with the requirement of Australian Standard 2432-1981. It was proposed that AS2432-1981 be voluntarily adopted by manufacturers in the first instance. As a result of the survey manufacturers were granted a twelve-month period of grace to ensure that their products were amended to meet the standard. A further survey of products on the market will be conducted to determine the need for introducing a mandatory standard under the Trade Practices Act.

11.   A revised children's nightwear safety standard to reduce the risk of burns and injuries to children caused by their night clothes catching fire was foreshadowed. The revised standard will prevent the use of certain highly flammable fabrics.

12.   Action was taken with regard to the sale of BMX bicycles which did not comply with the mandatory consumer product safety standard under the Trade Practices Act. The TPC decided not to prosecute on the condition that the retailer would effect a full public recall and ensure that adequate internal procedures were put in place to prevent a recurrence.

13.   In September 1983 the TPC issued a press release warning of the dangers associated with certain manually-operated winches. Following investigations by the TPC, the supplier of a winch which had failed in use placed recall notices relating to two models in newspapers throughout Australia. The TPC contacted suppliers of suspect brands, asking that they verify the claimed capacity or withdrew doubtful winches from the market place.

b) Protection of the consumers economic interest

Proposed Insurance Legislation

14.   Bills based on two reports of the Australian Law Reform Commission were introduced into the Senate in December 1983. The Bills, the Insurance (Agents and Brokers) Bill and the Insurance Contracts Bill were allowed to lie on the table to enable public comment on them.

15.   The Insurance (Agents and Brokers) Bill is aimed at regulating the activities of life and general insurance agents with a view to strengthening the financial stability of the industry overall; protecting the insuring public against the negligence or misconduct of an agent or broker; minimising practices harmful to the insuring public; and maintaining standards of conduct of, and the quality and service offered by, agents and brokers.

16.   The Insurance Contracts Bill is to implement the major reforms proposed by the Law Reform Commission Report entitled "Insurance Contracts". The proposals relate to the insurance contract itself, including the negotiations leading to its being made, and the parties' rights under it. In broad terms, the Bill is intended to improve the flow of information between the insurer and the insured and to provide a uniform and fair set of rules to govern the relationship between the insurer and the insured.

Electronic Funds Transfer Systems

17.   In recent years the growth and impact of electronic funds transfer systems (EFTS) has increased greatly in Australia. In September 1983 the Standing Committee of Consumer Affairs Ministers identified several consumer concerns and called on the Commonwealth Government to establish a task force to examine the need for legislation to protect EFTS users.

Petroleum Pricing

18.   In September 1983 the Standing Committee of Consumer Affairs Ministers called on the Commonwealth to convene a conference of Ministers responsible for petroleum prices to address problems related to the marketing of petroleum. (Arising out of this call, the Prices Surveillance Authority was directed in April 1984 to conduct a public inquiry into petroleum products pricing).

Report on Automotive Spare Parts Industry

19.   In October 1983 the Standing Committee of Consumer Affairs Ministers approved the release of a report by the TPC into pricing practices in the automotive spare parts industry. The Report outlined the findings of earlier inquiries into the price and quality of spare parts, gave an account of the industry and examined its supply and distribution systems. It also explored the ways in which manufacturers, suppliers and resellers established their prices.

20.   The Report concluded with a number of suggestions for possible Government action including:

    -- Abolition of recommended prices;

    -- Price control or surveillance;

    -- Reduction of functional distribution levels to contain costs and price; and

    -- Greater guidance to consumers.

Consumer Affairs Ministers will further consider the Report in the light of comments which have been sought from interested parties.

Food and Beverages

21.   The TPC carried out investigations in relation to misdescription and misleading labelling of certain foods and beverages. Several court actions resulted.

22.   In a press release dated 3rd October 1983, the TPC expressed concern about the pressures exerted on retailers by certain liquor industry groups in Victoria who were anxious to keep up the price of beer.

Travel

23.   Consumer complaints during the year about travel reflected the increased importance of the area and covered various problems, e.g. price increases arising from changes in currency relationships, piecemeal alteration of tours, breakdown in land transport arrangements.

24.   Airline overbooking is a long-standing issue. The crucial consideration is the lack of warning given to international air travellers that a confirmed reservation does not necessarily guarantee a seat on a particular flight and that such conduct may constitute misleading or deceptive conduct under the Trade Practices Act. The TPC approached international airlines operating in Australia about this issue and most airlines have accepted the need to provide warnings.

25.   At a meeting of the Standing Committee of Consumer Affairs Ministers in September 1983 Ministers agreed in principle to the introduction of uniform legislation to regulate travel agents. Ministers accepted proposals by a Working Group of Consumer Affairs and Tourism officers for a system of regulation incorporating licensing of travel agents, the establishment of a compensation fund, and the maintenance of trust accounts or the provision of bonds or bank guarantees. In October 1983 the Working Group released a discussion paper for comment by interested parties. (In March 1984 the Working Group reported back to Ministers recommending a comprehensive legislative package. Ministers agreed on a regulatory scheme which involves both Commonwealth and State legislation covering different aspects, and shared administration with the emphasis on State administration.)

Business Schemes

26.   The TPC issued a brochure on Franchising in June 1983 which set out a checklist which a potential investor could follow. The TPC has also instituted several court cases which should highlight the dangers of certain business schemes as well as providing a deterrent to those who might be tempted to operate fraudulent schemes.

27.   The TPC issued two media releases during the year warning small businessmen to guard against bogus demands for money. Demands have been made for money for advertising that is neither authorised nor approved beforehand.

The problem arises because many businessmen are apparently prepared to pay accounts on receipt of an invoice without checking whether they have in fact authorised the particular advertisement.

28.   During the year, the TPC received an increasing number of complaints concerning the country of origin displayed on a range of consumer goods. One such matter was taken to court.

2. Consumer Information

a) Labelling

29.   In August 1983 the Government released a Report on the uniformity of packaging and labelling legislation in Australia. The Report found that, while much had been done to progress uniformity among States, areas of non-uniformity still existed. Progress towards greater uniformity of packaging and labelling among the State and the Commonwealth is continuing.

i) Compulsory Labelling

30.   The requirements for flammability labelling of children's nightwear under the Trade Practices Act were amended in December 1983 to incorporate changes to the Australian Standard.

31.   In December 1983, the Minister altered the standard required under the Trade Practices Act for Care Labelling of Clothing, Household Textiles, Furnishings, Upholstered Furniture, Bedding, Piece Goods and Yarns. The new standard incorporates Australian Standard 1957-1982, which includes provision for skin and hide products.

b) Comparative testing

32.   The Australian Consumers' Association, which is an independent, non-profit organisation, publishes Choice Magazine. In 1983, Choice published the results of comparative tests on the quality and performance of many consumer goods and services including home computers, baby food, children's shoes and pest control.

3. Consumer education

33.   During the year, the TPC commenced a low cost experiment in consumer education. The experiment commenced with presentations by an officer on talk-back radio shows and also included the provision of articles for newspapers.

34.   During 1983, the TPC conducted a warranty review programme aimed at ensuring that suppliers understand their obligations under the Trade Practices Act and that the documents used by companies in consumer transactions reflect the requirements of the law. Problems have occurred with warranties and guarantees which attempt to exclude, limit or vary statutory conditions and

warranty rights given under the Act. In some cases manufacturers have also been found to mislead consumers about the extent of their rights under the Act. This usually occurs because many manufacturers and retailers are unaware of their obligations. In an effort to overcome this problem the TPC issued an Information Circular, "Consumer Protection: An Explanation of Statutory and Voluntary Guarantees and Warranties" and a Small Business brochure covering the matter.

35.   During the year, small business guidance work was given a high priority within the overall guidance programme of the TPC. Emphasis was placed on giving talks to meetings organised by small business associations or industry groups and to students.

36.   Three Small Business Brochures were issued during the year, bringing the total issued so far to eight. The new brochures covered the following topics:

-- The Practices Commission (An Introduction);

-- Recommended Prices;

-- Franchising.

The TPC recently released a new booklet entitled "Small Business and the Trade Practices Act".

4. Redress and Complaints Facilities

37.   For the 12 months ending 30th June 1983, consumer affairs authorities throughout Australia received 65 378 formal complaints representing a decrease of 5 per cent over the previous financial year.

38.   Despite this drop there were 75 per cent more complaints about real estate and accommodation in 1982-83 (14.5 per cent) than in the previous year. This increase coincided with the first full year of operation of the Victorian Residential Tenancies Tribunal, one of the State, Territorial and Commonwealth bodies to which complaints are made.

39.   The next most significant group of complaints concerned the purchase and repair of electrical goods (10.9 per cent), followed by used car purchases (9.1 per cent) and semi professional and other services (8.7 per cent). Statistics on reasons for complaint showed that 41.6 per cent claimed that the products or services had been unsatisfactory and 27.3 per cent alleged unfair or unfulfilled contracts.

III. RELATIONS BETWEEN CONSUMER POLICY AND OTHER ASPECTS OF
GOVERNMENT POLICY

40.   The Consumer Policy Branch of the Department of Home Affairs and Environment provided advice to other Departments on a number of matters during the year which, while not directly consumer policy matters, had obvious

implications for consumers. These matters included a universal health insurance scheme (Medicare), regulation of insurance intermediaries, legislation relating to insurance contracts and regulation of travel agents.

IV. GENERAL REMARKS

41.   In May 1983 the TPC issued a paper entitled "Public Discussion Paper on Future Directions of TPC Consumer Protection Work". The paper outlined several proposed programmes designed to enhance the TPC's consumer protection work. Comments on the paper were sought from interested persons and industry and consumer organisations. The TPC did not intend this as a once-only exercise; it hopes to establish and develop links which would ensure that its consumer protection work programme continues to take proper account of community views.

42.   In October 1983 the TPC outlined the programme it proposes to adopt. In order of priority, its areas of work will cover:

-- Enforcement -- continuing with existing work on industry and selling practices;

-- Research on industry self-regulation;

-- Further business guidelines -- covering the promotion and advertising of insurance and savings;

-- Survey of consumer attitudes; and

-- Consumer information -- exploring and developing the "Shoppers Rights" theme in co-operation with other consumer authorities.

43.   The National Consumer Affairs Advisory Council advises the Minister for Home Affairs and Environment on matters relating to Commonwealth responsibilities in consumer affairs. The Council is a non-Government body and its membership includes persons with backgrounds in consumer affairs, industry, trade unions and government. Topics considered by the Council in 1983 included amendments to the Trade Practices Act, insurance contracts, establishment of a national consumer education foundation and voluntary codes of conduct for business.

Part II

STATES AND TERRITORIES

I. INSTITUTIONAL DEVELOPMENTS IN THE FIELD OF CONSUMER POLICY

New South Wales

44.   The functions of the Prices Commission were expanded to include milk pricing and general price surveillance, leading to requests for justification of prices where appropriate.

45.   Major structural reorganisation was undertaken in order to provide more effective machinery for the adoption of an active preventative role. This is considered an appropriate development in the functions of the agency from the primarily reactive role that was adopted during the 70s.

Victoria

46.   In September 1982, the Minister of Consumer Affairs commissioned the Victorian Public Service Board to conduct a Review of the Ministry of Consumer Affairs.

47.   The Report of the Review, released in February 1983, contained the following major recommendations:

-- The Ministry should embrace as its primary objective the creation of fair market places for goods and services via adoption of the following operational strategies:

-- Regulatory activity to ensure that codes of conduct are established, observed and modified to reflect the changing environment; where appropriate to implement positive regulation through legislation;

. Remedial activity to ensure that consumers have appropriate avenues for redress;

. Educational activity to ensure that the operations of markets and the ethical standards consistent with fair markets are understood by the participants in the markets;

. Information-giving activity to ensure that consumers have sufficient information to be able to operate in the market on an equal footing with traders.

-- The Ministry should develop an appropriate policy formulation capacity which would include continuous monitoring of the environment, developing effective links with external interest groups (including industry and commerce, consumer groups, community groups, unions and the like) and providing appropriate consultative mechanisms to enable external input into the development of policy initiatives.

-- The Ministry's consumer education activities should be strengthened and aimed at specific markets and disadvantaged groups. Networks should be established with Government, community, trader and other organisations (accompanied by an appropriate grants programme) to facilitate education activities.

-- The Ministry's accesibility to the community should be improved by physical relocation of the Ministry to more appropriate premises, the development of a programme for the regionalisation of services, the establishment of a Customer Information Unit serviced by a computerised data base and an improved telephone system to provide better access.

-- The Consumer Affairs Bureau, Residential Tenancies Bureau and the complaint handling activities of the Motor Car Traders Committee should be replaced by a Conciliation Branch which would give emphasis to the conciliation of disputes between consumers and traders.

-- Dispute adjudication activities should be consolidated into a single Tribunal which would have a jurisdication covering the full range of disputes arising from transactions in the market place. Similarly, it was recommended that there be a single licensing authority rather than a proliferation of single purpose authorities.

-- The Ministry's activities in law enforcement and regulation should be strengthened, and industry self regulation encouraged where appropriate. Emphasis on the establishment of product (including product safety) and packaging standards should be increased.

48. An implementation Committee was constituted and one of its first priorities was to establish and set in place a new senior management and divisional structure.

49. While the primary emphasis has been on internal change, the Ministry commissioned two discussion papers on the purposes, objectives and future directions of the Ministry and consultation and community involvement with the Ministry. These papers were combined in a single discussion paper, which was then widely circulated for comment.

50. The final results of the consultation are to be referred to the Minister of Consumer Affairs for consideration and action regarding Consumer Affairs policies and priority consumer issues for Victoria.

51. A central recommendation of the Review into the Ministry was that the Consumer Affairs Council be replaced by a new body, the Victorian Consumer Affairs Committee. The Consumer Affairs Committee Act therefore abolished the Council and provided for a Committee of at least 9 persons to be appointed by the Minister. Its functions are to advise the Minister on any matters he might refer to it. To this end, the Committee can consult with or receive submissions from any persons or conduct any enquiries it deems necessary.

Queensland

52. Amendments to the Consumer Affairs Act 1970-1983 provided for the

setting up of a Product Safety Committee, to advise the Minister responsible for Consumer Affairs on matters of product safety and the sale of goods.

II. REGULATORY OR OTHER ACTION CONCERNING CONSUMER PROTECTION, INFORMATION AND EDUCATION, AND MEANS OF REDRESS

1. Consumer protection

a) Physical protection (product safety)

Victoria

53.   The Consumer Affairs (Product Safety) Act 1983, which came into operation on 1st February 1984, allows the Ministry of Consumer Affairs to prohibit the sale and distribution of dangerous consumer goods either on an interim basis (28 days) or permanently.

New South Wales

54.   The sale of the "Bodum Rio 8" jug, inflatube modular air bed, and certain spring loaded pop guns were prohibited.

55.   New safer goods regulations were introduced for bean bags and dust masks, and revised regulations were brought into effect for kerosene room heaters.

South Australia

56.   Under the Trade Standards Act, 1979, safety standards were issued for cosmetic products and erasers.

Queensland

57.   The Consumer Affairs Regulations were amended to include safety provisions for bean bags and construction requirements for pedal bicycles. The Regulations concerning pedal bicycles complement existing federal legislation.

b) Protection of the consumers economic interest

Queensland

58.   The Loan Fund Companies Act 1982 introduced major controls over the operation of loan fund companies.

23

South Australia

59. The Builders Licensing Act was amended to provide a framework for the introduction of a building indemnity scheme. This scheme provides for compulsory insurance to cover financial loss to consumers arising from defective workmanship or materials, or from failure to complete work in relation to the building of or alteration to a house if the builder dies, disappears or becomes insolvent.

60. Parliament passed a new Act providing for continuous licensing of second-hand motor vehicle dealers, more stringent licensing criteria, a more flexible penalty system and a compensation fund for satisfying claims of consumers.

New South Wales

61. Development of uniform model credit legislation with Victoria was completed to enable legislation to be introduced early in 1984.

62. The Consumer Credit Act was proclaimed in part to enable the Credit Tribunal to exercise powers relating to moratoria on home finance contracts.

2. Consumer Information

a) Labelling

i) Compulsory labelling

Victoria

63. The Consumer Affairs (Item Pricing) Bill 1983 was introduced into Parliament. The Bill will ensure the retention of item price marking in large self service supermarkets which introduce electronic checkout systems.

South Australia

64. Under the Trade Standards Act, 1979, an information standard was issued for solid chlorine (swimming pool) compounds.

Northern Territory

65. Date-marking regulations were enacted pursuant to the Weights and Measures (Packaged Goods) Act. The regulations provide for the date-marking of pre-packaged goods and came into effect as of 1st January 1983.

ii) Non-compulsory labelling

New South Wales

66.   An inter-Departmental committee was established to co-ordinate activity
on packaging and labelling matters between the Health, Agriculture, Industrial
Relations and Consumer Affairs Department.

3. Consumer Education

67.   The States and Territories continued their consumer information and
education programmes. These included:

-- Publication of pamphlets, brochures and posters;

-- Consumer education kits for schools;

-- Radio talk-back programmes and television segments;

-- Newspaper articles

-- Talks to schools and groups;

-- Films on specific topics;

-- Displays at shopping and community centres.

68.   In South Australia a second Consumer Education Training Course was conducted during the year and a publication which provides a comprehensive and
current resource package to teachers of consumer education was distributed to
all schools and most tertiary institutions.

AUSTRIA

I. INSTITUTIONAL DEVELOPMENTS IN THE FIELD OF CONSUMER POLICY

1.   One of the results of the Federal Parliament election of April 1983 was the creation of a new Federal Ministry for Family, Youth and Consumer Protection. In this way the concentration of relevant governmental and administrative tasks should be strengthened and the institutional basis for successful family and consumer policy should be laid.

2.   While consumer policy and consumer protection was not attributed to a specific section, it is now laid down legally that consumer policy including consumer protection (so far as it is not concentrated in the sphere of the Federal Ministry for Justice), the co-ordination of consumer policy including consumers' complaints, matters for the Consumers Advisory Board and those of protection against dangerous products, belong to the sphere of the Federal Ministry for Family, Youth and Consumer Protection.

3.   The section that dealt with consumer policy tasks in the Federal Ministry for Commerce, Trade and Industry has now been taken over from the new Ministry and continues its work under the Federal Ministry for Family, Youth and Consumer Protection. The former Consumer Advisory Board in the Federal Ministry for Commerce, Trade and Industry has finished its activities and has been reconstituted in the new ministry. In addition, the Product Safety Advisory Board, by virtue of the new Product Safety law, was established.

4.   The membership of the government authorities in the Association for Consumers' Information (Verein für Konsumenteninformation) under the aegis of the Federal Ministry for Commerce, Trade and Industry has also been taken over from the new Ministry. The budget is subventioned by the new Federal Ministry.

5.   In the framework of the Consumer's Advisory Board, two new working groups took up their activities: the first one "Credit Institutes and Consumers" works on standard conditions for current accounts. The second one "Technological Developments and Consumers" deals with problems of EAN (European Article Numbering) and scanners cashdesks. Another new working group was assigned for specific study of the problem of "bus tours".

6.   In addition, a "De-regulation" Committee was set up for the control of efficiency and necessity of ordinances in the field of consumer protection. Another new working group "Procedure Primer" met for the first time. This group will prepare the text of an information brochure for consumers involved in litigation.

II. REGULATIONS OR OTHER ACTION CONCERNING CONSUMER PROTECTION, INFORMATION AND EDUCATION AND MEANS OF REDRESS

1. Physical protection

7.   The new Product Safety Act (Federal law on the protection against dangerous products) came into force on 3rd September, 1983. The aim of the law is comprehensive protection against dangerous products by means of general standards, which can be applied in cases where, in specific branches, adequate protective measures are missing or insufficient.

8.   The law contains a list of protective measures, the instruments for applying these measures and the obligation to create an Advisory Board in charge of preparing expert opinions on the implementation of measures, advising the Federal Minister and exchanging data on dangerous products. The catalogue of possible measures which can be taken by the competent Federal Ministry after consultation with the Product Safety Advisory Board includes, e.g. instructions for use, packaging or performance requirements, advertising rules for the product, limitations of sale and warning references.

9.   The administrative authorities, the federal police authorities, all directorates of public hospitals, state-authorized laboratories, etc. have to communicate immediately any observations on dangerous products to the Federal Ministry for Family, Youth and Consumer Protection.

2. Consumer information

    a) Labelling requirements

10.   The following requirements concerning the labelling of consumer goods were issued in 1983:

-- Regulation of the Federal Minister of Commerce, Trade and Industry concerning the marking of electric household laundry driers (Fed. Law Gaz. No 38/1983);

-- Ordinance of the Federal Minister of Commerce, Trade and Industry on the marking of colour television sets (Fed. Law Gaz. No 39/1983);

-- Ordinance of the Federal Minister for Commerce, Trade and Industry concerning labelling of gas household-water-heaters (Fed. Law Gaz. No 491/1983).

    b) Other information activities

11.   The "No advertising material" campaign ("Bitte kein Reklame-Material"), which has been carried out since July 1980 together with the professional association of the advertising industry in the Federal Chamber of Commerce has been slightly modified with regard to the distribution of these stickers. It now takes place by means of post-office boxes, because the former method of delivery led to excessive stress on the personnel of both organisations.

12. In 1983 the legal Group of the Standing Committee on Travel agency questions dealt with 214 complaints. Italy headed the countries with most of the complaints, followed by Spain.

13. The number of consultations of the Information Centres of the Association for Consumer Information (Verein für Konsumenteninformation) is still increasing in Vienna, Innsbruck, Linz and Eisenstadt.

14. The Salzburg Chamber of Labour organized an exhibition on household accidents, which informed consumers on the various dangers of electrical appliances, fire and poison. Other crucial points of the exhibition programme concerned poisonous flowers and mushrooms, dangerous utensils for the garden and poisonous household waste.

III. RELATIONS BETWEEN CONSUMER POLICY AND OTHER ASPECTS OF GOVERNMENTAL POLICY

15. The monthly, specific price-control campaigns concerned various kinds of sausages in food stores, cold-storage plants, washing-machines and TV service, as well as the observance of price-labelling in florist shops. There followed the price control of car accessories, of alcoholic and non-alcoholic drinks, bakery products in restaurants and discotheques, on certain services of laundries and on consumer prices for liquid gas and car radios. Like every year, instead of price investigation of specific products, in December an intensive control of prices was carried out in the main shopping streets.

BELGIUM

I. INSTITUTIONAL DEVELOPMENTS IN THE FIELD OF CONSUMER POLICY

1.   Since its creation in December 1978 under the Trade Department of the Ministry of Economic Affairs, the Inspectorate-General for Consumer Policy is still the administrative body responsible for consumer policy, working through its two directorates: "General Problems and Credit" and "Consumer Information and Protection".

II. NEW REGULATIONS OR AMENDMENTS TO EXISTING LEGISLATION AND OTHER IMPORTANT MEASURES ADOPTED BY THE GOVERNMENT IN THE VARIOUS FIELDS

1. Consumer protection

a) Health and safety

2.   Several royal and ministerial decrees have laid down specific regulations to protect the consumer on clearly defined points:

-- 11th January 1983: Royal Decree supplementing that of 11th January 1982 concerning the marketing of sneezing-powders (Moniteur Belge of 1st February 1983);

-- 17th March 1983: Royal Decree laying down the methods of analysis to determine the presence of vinyl chloride in materials and objects intended to come into contact with foodstuffs, and the quantities of vinyl chloride given up to the foodstuffs by the materials and objects (Moniteur Belge of 19th May 1983);

-- 8th June 1983: Royal Decree concerning the production and marketing of dressed meat and meat preparations (Moniteur Belge of 20th July 1983);

-- 21st June 1983: Royal Decree laying down valid reference methods of analysis to monitor purity standards for additives (Moniteur Belge of 9th September 1983);

-- 12th July 1983: Changes in the lists of additives and pesticide residues authorised in foodstuffs (Moniteur Belge of 23rd September 1983);

-- 4th August 1983: Royal Decree concerning foodstuffs intended for special diets (Moniteur Belge of 30th December 1983);

-- 28th December 1983: Act on the sale of spirits (alcoholic drinks) and on the licence tax (Moniteur Belge of 30th December 1983).

3.   Several ministerial decrees have been published concerning the prohibition of marketing of electrical appliances. The texts have been circulated to Members of the Consumer Policy Committee as part of the exchange of information concerning consumer protection:

-- 3rd May 1983: an adaptor for American plugs and two socket outlets for three phase current (Moniteur Belge of 25th May 1983);

-- 17th May 1983: 17 electrical appliances such as mobile sockets, plugs and multi-socket mobile multi-socket blocks and dividing boxes (Moniteur Belge of 31st May 1983);

-- 12th July 1983: a radiator and a lighting fitting (Moniteur Belge of 20th August 1983);

-- 5th September 1983: two series of storage heaters (Moniteur Belge of 18th October 1983).

Also in the field of consumer health and safety, a Royal Decree of 13th September, which appeared in the Moniteur Belge of 25th October 1983, amended the general regulations concerning electrical installations.

b) Protection of consumers' economic interests:

4.   Various decrees concerning the price of certain commodities, objects or services have been passed.

2. Information and education of consumers

5.   As concerns information display, the Act of 14th November 1983 amending that of 14th July 1971 on Trade Practices stipulates that the price or charge indicated must be the total price or charge to be paid by the consumer, including VAT and all other taxes due, as well as the cost of all the services to be paid as a supplement by the consumer. The importance of this amendment in various sectors of the economy deserves to be emphasized. This Act entered into force on 1st January 1984.

6.   Comparative tests of products or services are recorded in the different monthly bulletins published by consumer organisations. These publications are mainly circulated among their members, although some are also available through traders. The consumer organisations are officially recognised by the authorities in that they are members of the Consumer Council, which is a consultative body under the supervision of the Minister for Economic Affairs.

7.   The Consumer Organisations' Research and Information Centre (CRIOC) set up in 1975 received a grant of BF 30 million in 1983 under the agreement on financial support concluded in January 1976 with the Ministry for Economic Affairs.

This public interest body has continued its activities by providing specialised assistance for consumer organisations through its three services dealing with research, information and education, and documentation, particularly by providing expert opinions on cases being dealt with by various national or international bodies: Consumer Council, Belgian Standards' Institute, EEC Economic and Social Committee, Consumer Contact Committee, etc. The influence of television advertising on child behaviour was the subject of a publication. As far as the education of young consumers in schools is concerned, the Centre has continued to aid teachers with their information and training activities and also to prepare teaching material and audio-visual programmes, the main focus being on children entering secondary education.

3. Appeals and claims procedures

8.   In the event of a dispute, the conciliation magistrate has jurisdiction when the sum involved is under BF 50 000, and the court of first instance when the sum is BF 50 000 or over.

9.   It should also be pointed out that the consumer associations have set up machinery for sectoral complaints, which will both respect the rights of all parties and also be quick and inexpensive. For example, one organisation has introduced this kind of machinery in agreement with the trade federations or associations in three sectors:

-- Furniture:

A standard contract has been drawn up with the association concerned for the use of traders who are members of this association, as well as other traders.

One of the clauses of this standard contract refers to the setting up of a commission for the settlement of disputes, comprising a neutral chairman, a lawyer representing the trade federation and another representing the consumers. This procedure starts with an attempt to come to an amicable arrangement. If this proves impossible, the Committee meets and, after hearing the parties, gives its decision. In the two years this system has existed, some fifty complaints have been dealt with, eight of which had to be settled by the Commission;

-- Travel:

The procedure is the same as for the furniture sector: standard contract drawn up with a trade federation and the (sectoral) Commission for settling disputes. Since September 1983, about a hundred complaints have been dealt with, for most of which an amicable arrangement was reached;

31

-- <u>Real-estate</u>:

A preliminary agreement of sale for the purchase of flats, houses and building land has been drawn up jointly, in particular with the <u>Federation Belge des Notaires</u> and the <u>l'Institut national du Logement</u>. This consumer organisation is aiming at the general introduction of this type of procedure, and another organisation has introduced a similar complaints procedure in the

-- <u>Textiles and dry-cleaning sector</u>:

If an amicable arrangement has not been reached between the consumer and the dry cleaner a Commission (comprising a Chairman, a Secretary from the trade organisation, an expert, three consumer members and three sectoral members) meets and examines the complaint. Some twenty cases are dealt with each month.

III. RELATIONS BETWEEN CONSUMER POLICY AND OTHER ASPECTS OF
GOVERNMENT POLICY

10. A Ministerial Decree of 22nd February 1982 imposed a general price freeze and a selective freeze was extended until the end of 1983.

11. Nine temporary laws were passed concerning house leases. In 1983 Act leases and other agreements regarding house possession came under the Act of 30th December 1982. This temporary law was rescinded by the Act of 29th December 1983, concerning contracts for renting real estate which amended a certain number of articles in the <u>Code Civil</u> and established permanent regulations in this connection. The Act of 29th December 1983 links rent changes with cost of living changes, according to a specified formula. The Act applies to all real estate. However, as far as its field of application is concerned, it should be noted that this text plays only a supplementary role where farm and commercial leases are concerned, and does not cover subsidised housing or shooting rights.

12. In order to promote energy conservation, the Government has taken various measures affecting the private consumer. Thus, following the setting up, within the Energy Department of the Ministry of Economic Affairs, of an "Energy Conservation Service", a campaign was launched with a view to informing and alerting the public with regard to the need to save energy.

13. Concerning energy conservation, a series of measures to limit energy consumption by private consumers have been taken. As well as the opportunity given the taxpayer (provided he is an owner-occupier) of deducting 40 per cent of any expenditure on thermal insulation from his total net taxable income (within certain limits), the Act of 28th December 1983 and the Royal Decree providing for its enforcement enable the taxpayer, whether he is the owner, owner-occupier, or tenant of the dwelling to deduct 20 per cent of his expenditure on renovation from his total income, also within certain limits. It should be pointed out that the <u>Société Nationale du Logement</u> applies standards for thermal insulation when subsidised housing is built.

14.   In the context of the legislation aimed at encouraging the rational use of energy, an Interdepartmental Committee for the Rational Use of Energy (CIPURE) has been set up, which will be responsible, among other things, for making quarterly comparative studies of demonstration, development and marketing projects.

CANADA

I. INSTITUTIONAL DEVELOPMENTS IN THE FIELD OF CONSUMER POLICY

1.   The transfer of the Metric Commission (responsible for Canada's metric conversion programme) to the department and the start-up of the UFFI Assistance programme (to supply information and financial assistance to owners of homes insulated with urea formaldehyde foam) account for apparent recent increases in the budget allocation of Consumer and Corporate Affairs Canada.

Expenditure and Person Year Allocation, 1979 to 1983

Consumer and Corporate Affairs Canada

Fiscal Year	Total Expenditures (constant 1981 dollars)	Person Years
1979-80	82 651 000	2 366
1980-81	78 213 000	2 316
1981-82	84 755 000	2 287
1982-83	134 757 000	2 537
1983-84	212 677 000	2 639

II. REGULATORY OR OTHER ACTION CONCERNING CONSUMER PROTECTION, INFORMATION AND EDUCATION, AND MEANS OF REDRESS

1.   Consumer Protection

a) Physical Protection (Product Safety)

i) Published Regulation

2.   A regulation was published in March 1983 banning the sale of booster cushions that do not meet a prescribed standard. Booster cushions enable children to use car seat belts, designed for adults, in a safe manner.

ii) Proposed Regulations

3.   Two proposed regulations were also published during the year. The first dealt with sneezing powders and increased the number of chemicals prohibited from inclusion in these products. The other is a proposal to regulate baby carriages and strollers (perambulators and push-chairs) and mandate safety standards for their performance. Regulations have also been proposed to limit the level of N-nitrosamines in baby bottle nipples and pacifiers.

iii) Product Recalls

4.   Three manufacturers of strollers instituted voluntary recalls on a number of models because of a pinching hazard which did not become apparent until some two years after manufacture. Other recalls included 1.7 million cigarette lighters imported from Mexico, and various brands of pacifiers (dummies) which did not comply with the appropriate regulations.

iv) Risk Assessment Study

5.   The development of a risk assessment model has been undertaken in order to assist in the determination of priorities and thus lead to a better use of resources. This initiative follows the establishment, in 1982, of an accident/injury reporting system (CAIRE) using data collected from five hospitals across Canada.

v) Scientific and Technical Research

6.   Research is being carried out in many scientific and technical areas related to hazardous consumer products. At the present time, considerable attention is given to the emission of formaldehyde gas from particle board and flammability with particular reference to the burning characteristics of upholstered furniture.

vi) Other

7.   A programme was developed in co-operation with retail trade associations to inform retailers of the dangers associated with solvent abuse to induce hallucinatory effects and the precautions that they should take in displaying and selling their products in order to minimise the chances of such abuse by children.

b) Protection of the Consumer's Economic Interest

i) Sale and Advertising of Gemstones

8.   A joint government/industry committee was created for the purposes of establishing voluntary guidelines with respect to the sale and advertising of gemstones.

ii) Misleading Advertising

9. Guidelines on How to Avoid Misleading Advertising have been published by Consumer and Corporate Affairs in order to synthesise articles and policy statements published previously in issues of the department's Misleading Advertising Bulletin.

Under the Combines Investigation Act, the description of which was provided in the 1981 report, a total of 265 cases relating to misleading advertising and deceptive marketing practices were considered by the courts during the year ending 31st December 1983. These consisted of 136 new proceedings commenced during the year and 129 carried over from previous years, 17 of which involved appeals from trial courts. Of those cases, 130 were concluded during the year with 115 resulting in convictions.

iii) Price of Pharmaceutical Products

10. Sub-section 41 4) of the Patent Act allows alternate, bio-equivalent products (generics) to enter the market and compete with the original patented product. This approach is unique to Canada and has served to moderate drug price increases, resulting in estimated savings to the consumer at between 150 and 200 million dollars per year, when compared to the prices of the same products in the United States. A review of the provision was conducted during 1983, which included discussions with companies, provinces, consumers and health professionals. The process identified that there is insufficient evidence on which to base a policy decision, that there is no consensus on what change should be made and that a great deal of concern exists regarding drug prices. As a result, a Commission of Inquiry has been established to look into all aspects of the industry and to recommend a course of action. At the same time discussions will be held with provinces regarding ways to influence drug costs. Both reports are expected by late 1984.

iv) Mortgages

11. In February 1984, the Government brought forward several proposals dealing with the mortgage market. First, amendments to the Interest Act were proposed which would give consumers the right to prepay their mortgages at any time with a limit on the size of the prepayment penalty, ensure complete disclosure of all terms and conditions relating to mortgages, and remove legal obstacles to the introduction of variable rate and index-linked mortgages. Second, a Mortgage Rate Protection Programme was proposed which is designed to enable consumers to purchase protection against extraordinary increases in mortgage rates. Third, proposals were made to facilitate the development of longer term mortgages through the introduction of mortgage-backed securities.

v) Pensions

12. In December 1983, a Parliamentary Task Force on Pension Reform released its final report. Subsequently, in February 1984, the Government of Canada put forward several proposals relating to this topic. Among these were several amendments to the Pension Benefits Standards Act designed to bring about significant reforms of minimum standards for private pension arrangements.

The particular issues addressed by these proposed amendments include inflation protection, vesting, portability, compulsory membership, and information disclosure. Complementary to this, proposals were made to change the tax assistance system with regard to pensions.

vi) Deposit Insurance

13.   Financial institutions which accept consumer deposits are generally members of the Canada Deposit Insurance Corporation. As of 17th January 1983, consumer deposits with these companies are insured to a maximum of $60 000 per person. Previously, the maximum was $20 000 per person.

2.   Consumer Information

a) Labelling

i) Compulsory Labelling

14.   The Energuide Programme which requires the labelling of all refrigerators, freezers, clothes washers, clothes dryers and dishwashers for energy consumption was maintained in operation during 1983. A new Directory containing up-to-date information on the energy consumed by every model of every appliance type available for sale in Canada was published during 1983. The programme is under evaluation and consideration will be given to its possible extension to other energy consuming appliances.

15.   Guidelines for food manufacturers and advertisers on the interpretation of the Food and Drugs Act and Regulations have been developed and will be issued in 1984. Proposals regarding labelling requirements for irradiated foods, non-retail containers and mineral water were submitted for public consultation.

16.   Consultations with interested parties were initiated on a number of commodity regulations (e.g. fur and chamois) under the National Trade Mark and True Labelling Act as part of the on-going Regulatory Reform process.

ii) Non-Compulsory Labelling

17.   The department agreed to provide the co-ordination relative to the preparation of industry guidelines for the use of the term "natural" in the labelling and advertising of foods. Responses to the initial proposal concerning nutrition labelling, as jointly issued by the Departments of Health and Welfare and Consumer and Corporate Affairs, have been received and will be evaluated during 1984.

b) Other Information Activities

i) Consumer Exhibitions

18.   Consumer Resource Expositions across Canada, and the publication of corresponding Consumer Resource Guides resulted in a greater awareness within government of consumer issues. Elected and appointed government officials and employees were the recipients of the information provided through the Expositions and Guides, which detailed the roles played by different government agencies in consumer-related services and programmes. One result has been more efficient handling of consumer inquiries by government.

ii) Publications

19.   In order to foster better understanding and informed debate of the problems encountered by consumers, Consumer and Corporate Affairs Canada has continued to sponsor research on various issues. The following reports have been published recently:

Making your Home Accessible: A Disabled Consumer's Guide	Carol Kushner Patricia Ladia Lalta Andrew Aitkens
Consumer Problems in the Automobile Repair Industry	Stephen E. Margolis
Consumer Bankrupts in Canada	J.W. Brighton J.A. Connidis
Issues Regarding the Reform of Canada's Private Pensions System	James E. Pesando
Regulation of the Canadian Life Insurance Market: Some Issues Affecting Consumers	G.F. Mathewson R.H. Winter C.J. Campbell T.K. Gussman
Products Liability and Personal Injury Compensation in Canada: Towards Integration and Rationalisation (Volume I)	E.P. Belobaba
Consumer Product Warranty Reform: Regulation in Search of Rationality (Volume II)	E.P. Belobaba
Exemptions Under the Canadian Copyright Act	Dennis N. Magnusson Victor Nabhan
Collective Agencies for the Administration of Copyright	Douglas A. Smith

4.   Redress and Complaints Facilities

a) Creation and Development of Small Claims Procedures and Similar Redress Facilities

20.   Consumer and Corporate Affairs Canada is undertaking an analysis of the cost-effectiveness of third party mediation and arbitration mechanisms as an alternative to consumers having to resort to the courts.   There is a growing interest in such alternatives in Canada.   The Canadian Council of Better Business Bureaux is implementing formal mediation and arbitration programmes.   The Canadian Bar Association has introduced two pilot projects that offer mediation and arbitration services.

b) Special Attention to "Vulnerable" Consumers

21.   A Vulnerable Consumer Programme which is designed to help resolve the consumer problems of special populations has recently been initiated.   This programme attempts to focus the resources of voluntary, business, and public sector organisations on the particular consumer concerns of such groups as the elderly, the disabled, native peoples and youth.

III. RELATIONS BETWEEN CONSUMER POLICY AND OTHER ASPECTS OF GOVERNMENTAL POLICY

1.   International Trade

i) Role of Consumer Policy Authorities

22.   In the recent world-wide economic recession, the problems of a few Canadian manufacturing industries were exacerbated by increases in imports. Consumer and Corporate Affairs Canada was one of the four economic policy departments primarily involved in the formulation of corresponding government actions.

ii) Role of Consumer Organisation

23.   The Minister of State (International Trade) has constituted advisory panels to advise him in matters respecting the administration of current restrictions on imports of clothing and footwear.   The Consumers' Association of Canada is among those groups requested to participate on these panels.

iii) Legislation

24.   In the review of Canadian import policy legislations consideration is being given to provisions which would allow account to be taken of the implications for consumers of anti-dumping actions.

iv) Other

25.   A discussion paper entitled <u>Canadian Trade Policy for the 1980s</u> was
published by the Government of Canada to enhance general awareness of the importance, to Canadian consumers and producers, of the multilateral trading
system and the associated policy issues.

2.   Competition

i) Combines Investigations

26.   It is anticipated that amendments to strengthen the <u>Combines Investigation Act</u> will be tabled in 1984. The proposals include changes to the merger,
monopoly and conspiracy provisions of the Act.

27.   Among current investigations, the public hearings concerning the state
of competition in the Canadian petroleum industry are particularly note-
worthy. It is expected that this examination, which encompasses the international, marketing, refining, production and pipeline aspects of the industry, will be completed in 1984.

ii) Airline Passenger Transportation

28.   A comprehensive review of the regulation (by the Government of Canada)
of domestic airline fares was initiated late in 1983. A "Panel" has been constituted by the Canadian Transport Commission and public hearings are to be
completed in April 1984.

iii) Telecommunications

29.   A decision of the Canadian Radio Television Commission in late 1982 allowed consumers to utilise their own telephones rather than those provided by
the telephone company. (Previously consumers were required to utilise at
least one telephone of the telephone company.) This decision set the stage
for the recent revision to the schedule of tariffs which reduced rates for
consumers who do <u>not</u> use terminal equipment available from the telephone
company.

iv) Broadcast Entertainment

30.   The range of broadcast signals available to consumers increased in
1983. In keeping with licenses granted by government, "Pay TV" became available to most Canadian consumers through cable television companies. In addition, decisions taken by the Canadian Radio-Television and Telecommunications
Commission in 1983 have enhanced access by consumers and broadcasters to
satellite transmission of television signals.

IV. GENERAL REMARKS

31.   Broad economic conditions in 1983 had important implications for consumer policy developments in Canada. In the aftermath of the world-wide economic downturn of 1982, large budgetary deficits have necessitated severe restraint in government programme expenditures. Concern for economic performance has prevented the expansion of some "social" programmes. In view of the
relatively high level of unemployment, employment generation (and preservation) has assumed a higher priority in economic policy formulation. One re-
flection of this situation has been a heightened sensitivity to the implicit
costs to the private sector of regulatory initiatives. As a result, regulation has generally been limited to the status quo apart from initiatives to
react to serious problems. Indeed, in the telecommunications area some deregulation has in effect taken place.

32.   The recent recession has occasioned a comprehensive review of government policy which is being carried out by the Royal Commission on the Economic
Union and Development Prospects for Canada (Macdonald Commission). In 1983,
Consumer and Corporate Affairs Canada made a formal submission to the Commission. Among the points made in this submission, the need for regular and open
review of domestic regulations governing market transactions and (tariff and
non-tariff) barriers to (international and intranational) trade was stressed.

DENMARK

I. INSTITUTIONAL DEVELOPMENTS IN THE FIELD OF CONSUMER POLICY

1.   There were no significant institutional developments during 1983 apart from the changes in the complaint boards mentioned under II, 1(b) and 4.   The work of the consumer institutions and consumer organisations was continued.

II. REGULATORY OR OTHER ACTION CONCERNING CONSUMER PROTECTION, INFORMATION AND EDUCATION, AND MEANS OF REDRESS

1. Consumer Protection

a) Physical protection (product safety)

2.   At the request of the various consumer organisations and institutions, the toy "The Wonderful Watersnake" has been withdrawn from the market, and warnings have been given of other articles like travelling beds, masks, lamp oil, illegal fire extinguishers and electrical heating pads.   In 1983, DEMKO (The Danish Board for Approval of Electrical Equipment) prohibited the sale and use of a certain electrical heating pad due to fire risk.

3.   The Danish National Food Institute has warned consumers about a number of foodstuffs which are dangerous to health, and the Institute has likewise taken action against the sale of dangerous food processors.   A pilot experiment regarding the EEC notification system on accidents caused by certain products -- outside of industry -- has been carried out in Denmark.

4.   Within the Nordic co-operation on consumer questions in-depth studies of the part textiles have played in connection with fires have been submitted.

5.   A COPOLCO(1) seminar on "Standards and Child Safety" was held in Copenhagen in April 1983 and within COPOLCO, action is being considered to immediately initiate the reduction of safety risks for children.

6.   Regulations have been adopted for an annual control and cleaning of gas water heaters and for use of UF-foam for insulating of cavities in buildings, and it has been decided to initiate a special control.

7.   The Ministry of the Environment on the 1st February issued a notice on raw materials, household appliances, machines, etc. used for food production.

8.   The Danish Standards Associations has established a committee to work out standards for bicycle seats and traffic reflexes.

b) Protection of the Consumers' Economic Interests

9.   The mandatory energy labelling system on the energy consumption of electric ovens is, according to an agreement between the Ministry of Energy and the Danish Institute for Informative Labelling, carried out by the latter.

10.   In 1983, the Consumer Ombudsman dealt with a number of cases within the fields of dangerous toys, sun lamps, marketing of bank services, misleading advertising regarding work done at home and job offers, mail-order sales, marketing of stamps and of undertakers. The Consumer Ombudsman has also examined the internal regulations for all credit card companies in pursuance of the Danish Marketing Practice Act, and the new regulations in the Act regarding credit purchases.

11.   The majority of the cases brought before the courts were cases on premium or similar inducements.

12.   The Consumer Complaints Board has taken over the complaints regarding some goods and services from private complaint boards, and thus increased its activities. The complaints board for radio and TV sets has ceased its activities due to economic difficulties in the trade organisations running the board.

13.   The number of complaints received by the Board has not been reduced, so the number of cases dealt with in writing is about 3000, and the Secretariat has dealt with about 15 000 enquiries in all.

14.   A mass media commission established by the Prime Minister's Department has submitted a report on the establishment of an additional TV program with or without advertising.

15.   On the 1st April, 1983 a new act on credit purchases was put into force. The purpose of the act is to increase consumer protection regarding credit purchases, and it includes regulations on information regarding the costs involved in credit purchasing, to prohibit mortgage and the use of bills of exchange. This act succeeds a former act on instalment credit.

16.   The Minister of Justice has introduced a bill on debt reorganisation. The bill will make it possible for persons deeply indebted to have their economy reorganised.

17.   The Minister of Industry has in 1983 introduced a bill on credit cards.

18.   The Nordic consumer and motor organisations, i.e. in Denmark the Consumer Council and FDM, worked out a common "Nordic Antirust Kodex".

19.   The Consumer Council and the organisation of estate agents have brought up the subject of a change in the commission agreement between consumer salesmen and real estate agents. Furthermore, negotiations have been initiated

with the Danish Insurance Association on the matter of claims for damages caused by natural catastrophes.

20.   The Ministry of Public Works has established a committee that has recently submitted a report introducing a cover-arrangement.

21.   A Committee under the Ministry of Justice has reported on the authorisation of repair shops.

22.   The Ministry of Housing has established a committee to work out rules for conditions in connection with changes of ownership.

2. Consumer Information

a) Labelling

23.   The Monopoly and Price Authority has prepared rules for price labelling in connection with the sale of beer and soft drinks, and for the display of price lists outside restaurants.

24.   The Supervision of Commercial and Savings Banks has issued an order regarding the quotation of fees for services rendered by financial institutes.

b) Comparative testing

24.   The Home Economic Council has done comparative tests within the field of household apparatus and devices, plants for house heating, spare time articles, textiles, chemical-technical articles and foodstuffs. Part of the studies has been done in co-operation with Nordic (NEK) and other European (European Testing Group) consumer institutions.

25.   The Consumer Council has in 1983 undertaken investigations of vitamin pills, frozen and fresh fish, baby clothing, bicycle safety helmets, and children's safety products. The results were published in "TENK".

26.   The Consumer Council has furthermore investigated and evaluated the standard conditions set up by financial institutes for certain types of loans.

27.   A NEK-project covers consumer problems and claims in connection with the use of data techniques in every-day commodity trade.

c) Advisory Services

28.   The Advisory Services of the Consumer Council and the Home Economic Council are still available both by telephone and by writing, by personal contact and via lectures. The Consumers' Council has a special complaint information service and, furthermore, information is given through local groups of consumers.

29.   The regular leaflets on price information published by the Monopoly and Price Authority were supplemented by a brochure about the price-labelling law.

d) Mass Media

30.   The Home Economic Council's publication "Advice and Results" is published 8 to 9 times yearly with a circulation of about 70 000 copies.
Furthermore the Economic Council also issues 4 new leafleats in 60 000 copies
yearly and a number of other publications.

31.   The Consumer Council's publication "TENK" is published 10 times annually with 30 000 copies and it has 20 000 subscribers.

e) Other information activities

32.   In 1983 the Consumer Council has published two guides, one entitled
"The Best for the Child", and the other was "How to Complain", in order to inform the public where and when to address the most common consumer complaints.

33.   The Consumer Council conducted a campaign for lead-free petrol in 1983.

34.   The Energy Saving Commission has been responsible for general
energy-saving campaigns.

35.   A tele-data experiment is being carried out.   It was started on the
30th March, 1982, and is to be continued until the 1st April, 1984.   By then,
600 private households will have participated in the experiment.

36.   In 1983, the State Information Service in co-operation with the Ministry of Justice issued several consumer publications on "Consumer Rights When
Buying on Credit" and "Consumer Purchase".

3. Consumer Education

37.   Within the NEK co-operation scheme, two publications have been issued
and a seminar on consumer journalism has been held.   Furthermore, a report on
"Consumer Education for School Teachers" has been submitted.

38.   In co-operation with the Royal Danish School of Educational Studies,
the Consumer Council continues pilot-projects on consumer education in three
schools in Copenhagen.

39.   Within NEK, a project on consumer questions regarding pre-schools,
day-care centres, kindergartens and the education of teachers in these institutions is being carried out.

40.   The Ministry of Education has arranged an international seminar on the
education of consumer guides.   The seminar was held on the 12th-17th February,
1984.

4. Redress and Complaints Facilities

41.   In Denmark, there is no special facility regarding small claims procedures and similar consumer redress.   Consumers with an income below certain
limits may, however, still upon application be granted "free action" for

bringing consumer questions to court. Consumers with an income above this limit have the possibility of getting the costs covered by private insurance.

42. Five authorised private complaint boards have ceased their activities with the exception of the Weekend Place Complaints Board. The activities of these boards are now being handled by the Consumer Complaints Board.

III. RELATIONS BETWEEN CONSUMER POLICY AND OTHER ASPECTS OF GOVERNMENTAL POLICY - THE HEALTH SECTOR

The "Prevention Council" established by the Ministry of the Interior has in 1983, among other things, submitted the report "Accidents due to Falls where Older Persons are Involved - Prevention by Means of Re-Arranging Domestic Interior Architecture".

NOTE AND REFERENCE

1. ISO -- Consumer Policy Committee.

FINLAND

I. INSTITUTIONAL DEVELOPMENTS IN THE FIELD OF CONSUMER POLICY

1.   No substantial organisational changes have occurred at ministerial level.

2.   The Council of State obliged four new consumer advisory areas to start consumer advisory services in 1983. When these services have been started, there will be altogether 46 municipal consumer advisers acting in 132 munici- palities. The number of inhabitants in these municipalities totals 2 800 000 persons, which is about 58 per cent of Finland's total population.

3.   A new Consumer Council was nominated by the Council of State after the parlimentary election in March 1983.

4.   A Finnish delegation was founded on the occasion of the "International Consumer Rights Day". The delegation will be liable for the preparations of the International Consumer Rights Day, which is celebrated every year on 15th March. The delegation was composed of representatives from the Household and Consumer Organisations, the Central Organisations of Wage and Salary Earners and the Consumer Authorities.

5.   The budget allocated to the National Board of Trade and Consumer Inte- rests (price and competition affairs included) for 1983 totalled Mk 18.8 mil- lion. The joint budget of the Consumer Ombudsman and the Consumer Complaints Board amounted to Mk 4.1 million. Municipal consumer counselling received Mk 1.8 million in government support. A sum of Mk 372 000 was granted to con- sumer organisations in government aid through consumer administration. Governmental aid to voluntary organisations is financed mainly from the funds of the Ministry of Education. Nearly all the allowances have increased com- pared with the previous year.

47

II. REGULATORY OR OTHER ACTION CONCERNING CONSUMER PROTECTION, INFORMATION AND EDUCATION, AND MEANS OF REDRESS

1. Consumer protection

a) Physical protection (product safety)

6.   As regards voluntary measures relating to product safety, the following standards and product declarations have been published for:

-- Structural and operational requirements for SFS electric safety switches;

-- SFS 4941 for electric and gas ranges. Attention was paid to children's safety;

-- SFS guide 1. Instructions for the use of certain consumer goods;

-- TSL 35-000. Coffee percolators.

7.   The Consumer Council has finished its Programme of Consumer Policy, which intends to give guidelines for the development of consumer policy. The Ministry of Trade and Industry has asked for opinions on the Programme for further measures.

8.   In March the Consumer Council handed its statement on consumer policy to the Council of State. The Council emphasized the necessity of protecting consumers against economic and health risks caused by faulty products. The Council also demanded that consumer research be developed, marketing directed towards children and young people be controlled more efficiently and consumer counseling be extended so as to cover the whole country. The Consumer Council demanded in general to develop administration of consumer affairs.

9.   In June the Consumer Council handed its statement on foodstuff policy to the authorities, research institutes and organisations concerned. On the same occasion the Council also delivered the report of a working group for foodstuffs.

-- Corrective action

10.   The National Board of Trade and Consumer Interests has put a ban on the sale of a toy called "Magic Egg" that was proved to be dangerous for children. The ban was intensified by confiscation. The Magic Egg contains a toy imitating a fish, a beetle, a snail, a cock, a hand, etc. According to the instructions for use the object shall be put into water. In three hours it will have swollen 20 times and in 24 hours 130 times bigger than its original size. If swallowed the toy will continue to swell and may choke the intestinal channel. In such a case the child must be operated upon urgently. The problem is that the toy is not visible in an X-ray screening.

11.   The Market Court ordered in its decision No. 1982:22 a Finnish company to alter its advertising by warning the consumers of the risks they may be exposed to when handling a gadget sold as an auxiliary device to a drilling

machine. According to the Market Court the warning note sent by the manufacturer had been dispatched after the time limit. The note had also contained advertising elements. As, in the Market Court's opinion, the manufacturer had neglected to fulfil his obligation in this respect, the Court decided that the fine of Fm 100 000 imposed on the manufacture because of his negligence of the said obligation shall be paid (No. 1983:7).

12.   The Consumer Ombudsman has forbidden the manufacturer of a certain type of whistle used for frightening elks away from highways to market the product as an "Elks Frightener" and to claim in advertisements that the whistle frightens elks, keeping them away from highways. The claim should not at all be used, unless it is scientifically and incontestably proved that the gadget does have such properties. The prohibition was reinforced by the imposition of a fine of Fk 100 000.

-- Research projects

13.   The following studies ordered by the National Board of Trade and Consumer Interests have been completed during the year under review:

14.   A study of the re-use of Consumer goods and of factors influencing consumers' attitudes toward second-hand goods has been conducted by the Research Centre of Household and Consumer Affairs.

15.   A study of special offers for everyday commodities was carried out for the purpose of investigating their advertising and consumers' attitudes towards such offers. The study was carried out by the Research Centre of Household and Consumer Affairs, and the Consumer Ombudsman's Office participated in its financing.

16.   A study of accidents and damages caused by various products was accomplished as far as the final stage of the final report. The study concentrated on examining what sort of accidents and damages to property different products may cause, and on evaluating the risk of damage inherent in these products. The study was carried out at the laboratory for industrial safety techniques of the State Technical Research Centre of Finland. It was financed, among others, by the Ministry of Justice, the Consumer Council and the State Technical Research Centre.

17.   A study called "Need, Commodity and the Social Association" dealt with the position and meaning of certain central factors in the creation of various needs. The study was carried out by the Workers' Economic Research Institute in Finland.

18.   A number of instructions for use for the most common household machines were investigated for the purpose of finding out the deficiencies, if any, in the text. The investigation was carried out by the Work Efficiency Association and the State Technical Research Centre for Agricultural Machines according to an agreed schedule of the division of work.

19.   The Foodstuffs Laboratory of the State Technical Research Centre has analysed the nutritional contents of 39 preparations sold in health food shops and regarded as the main source of certain substances.

20.   Furthermore several studies concerning foodstuffs have been completed

during the year under review by the National Board of Trade and Consumer Interests.

21.   The Household Division of the Work Efficiency Association has tested washing machines, refrigerators and electric ranges of different makes. The Association has also examined the consumption of warm water in apartment houses and the standard of living of older people from the point of view of their physical housing conditions. In addition the Association has examined the functioning of the small houses built in Torpparinmäki -- a new residential area near Helsinki -- according to new energy-saving plans.

22.   The Research Centre of Household and Consumer Affairs has published two studies concerning washing spaces.

23.   The State Research Centre of Agricultural Machines has made a group test of dishwashers. The Centre has also tested different central heating boilers and investigated various forms of energy consumption in owner-occupied houses.

24.   In addition consumer authorities have participated in several Nordic research projects.

b) Protection of the consumers' economic interest

25.   The regulations concerning marketing practices for houses and flats entered into force on 1st January 1984. The provisions of the Consumer Protection Act concerning marketing and the control of contractual terms have been extended to apply to the offering for sale, sale and other marketing of houses and flats as well. The act concerning the marketing practices for houses contains detailed regulations of the information that must be given to the consumer when houses and flats are marketed.

26.   The amendments made to the regulations concerning pharmaceutical preparations and foodstuffs entered into force at the beginning of July. The purpose of the amendments is to make it easier for consumers to buy preparations which have a reduced effect compared with ordinary pharmaceutical preparations but which relieve and prevent pains, and to exempt a number of medical preparations containing less medical drugs from a time-consuming registration. The amendments also make it possible to declare the medicinal use of certain foodstuffs and cosmetic preparations on their packages or in marketing.

27.   The Consumer Council took a stand on the practice of marking prices and unit prices on products. The report was submitted to the Central Committee of Commerce and to the National Board of Trade and Consumer Interests.

28.   In its letter of 15th June addressed to organisations of motor car dealers, the stations testing used motor cars, the Ministry of Trade and Industry and other consumer authorities, the Consumer Council proposed that measures be taken to reduce the problems relating to the purchase of a second-hand car.

29.   The Consumer Ombudsman published the principles according to which claims concerning energy-savings shall be evaluated by virtue of the Consumer Protection Act.

30.   The Market Court has, at the request of the Consumer Ombudsman, forbidden the marketing of a repair commitment including a certain responsibility on the client's part, because the commitment was marketed as a guarantee. In addition, the Market Court considered it unreasonable, from the consumer's point of view, that a guarantee implies responsibility on the consumer's part. Nos. 1983:2, 1983:12.

-- Contractual relations

31.   The Consumer Ombudsman and the Confederation of Finnish Industries have worked out model terms for guarantees granted for new consumer goods. The firm giving the guarantee may use the model terms by specifying the product and completing the terms with information about the person or firm giving the guarantee and the guarantee period. He may also specify those parts of goods that are or are not covered by the guarantee. The principles of model terms shall in no case be interpreted to the detriment of the client.

32.   The Consumer Ombudsman and the National Board of Post and Telecommunications have agreed on revised terms of accession for new telephone subscribers. The negotiations were based on terms agreed upon previously with the Association of Private Telephone Companies in Finland and on corresponding terms applied in Sweden.

2. Consumer Information

a) Labelling

i) Compulsory labelling

33.   An act concerning the declaration of the country of origin of consumer goods entered into force on 1st January 1984. The act applies to such consumer goods as are intended to be sold for private consumption in Finland. A corresponding decree specifies the consumer goods for which such declaration is compulsory. The regulations are also applied to non-conpulsory declaration of the country of origin. The act is, however, not applicable to foodstuffs or second-hand consumer goods.

34.   The National Board of Health has issued a decision concerning the composition and the instructions for use of baby foods and infant formulae (450/83).

35.   The National Board of Trade and Consumer Interests has given a new decision on marketable mushrooms (644/83). The decision contains regulations concerning the offering for sale of mushrooms and their commercial names. The regulations concerning quality classification are a new element in the decision.

ii) Non-compulsory labelling

36.   The National Board of Trade and Consumer Interests has sent a circular concerning the supervision of expressions used on packages and in the marketing of foodstuffs, which are governed by the Act on Foods.

51

b) Comparative testing

37.   The Household Division of the Work Efficiency Association conducted in Autumn 1983 a comparative test of 12 microwave ovens. The test concentrated on measuring the input and the microwave power, the utilisation ratio and the evenness of the heating process when foods of different types and forms are baked or roasted in the oven.

38.   The laboratory for industrial safety techniques of the State Technical Research Centre has tested 15 different vacuum cleaners for the purpose of measuring the purity of outgoing air.

39.   The Research Centre for Household and Consumer Affairs has performed a comparative test of irons. The test was financed by the National Board of Trade and Consumer Interests.

c) Advisory services

40.   In densely populated areas the main part of advisory services consists of giving advice to individual consumers in different problematic situations. The need for preventive advisory services has become more and more obvious. In order to make it easier for consumer advisers to spread information, plans have been made for general information campaigns. In 1983 the main emphasis was put on problems relating to the purchase of a second-hand car and how to prevent such problems.

41.   In 1983 the consumer advisers were consulted 50 385 times. 69 per cent of the contacts were complaints. The consumer advisers arranged a total of 1 124 informative meetings, which were attended by 28 218 persons, and 58 exhibitions, which were visited by 111 434 persons. Besides these, approximately 35 000 complaints were settled by the municipal consumer advisers at local level.

d) Mass media

42.   The National Board of Trade and Consumer Interests has published six issues of Kuluttajatietoa (Consumer Information) and several issues of an informative leaflet called The Department of Consumer Affairs Informs. Reports of recent tests and studies were given in Publications from the Department of Consumer Affairs. A guide called "Kuluttajan ABC" (The Consumers's ABC) which deals with the rights and obligations of the consumers was completed.

43.   An information campaign directed to those planning to buy a second-hand car was launched. Of the measures taken within the framework of the campaign may be mentioned an informative spot transmitted in MTV (the Finnish commercial television company). Various proposals for suitable headings were also distributed to the press.

44.   The consumer protection authorities (The Consumer Ombudsman's office and the Consumer Complaints Board) have published four issues of Kuluttajansuojalehti (Consumer Protection Magazine) and several information leaflets. Two brochures on motor cars have also been published: one dealing with car repairs and the other giving advice to consumers planning to buy a

second-hand car. The Consumer Ombudsman's Office has worked out a leaflet containing the Consumer Protection Act and examples of its application in a number of cases. The leaflet, which has been sent to professionals of advertising and marketing, had in fact been drawn up to look like an advertisement.

e) Other information activities

45. A circulating exhibition called Hengari and informing consumers of various things relating to the care and purchase of clothes was arranged for consumer advisers, schools and other educational institutes.

46. The Household and Consumer Organisations, the Central Organisations of Wage and Salary Earners and the consumer authorities participated in the planning and celebration of the International Consumer Rights Day.

47. The National Board of Trade and Consumer Interests arranged a seminar on the use of second-hand goods. The seminar discussed, among other things, whether it is possible to prolong the lifetime of commodities in general and to reduce the amount of garbage.

48. Another seminar was arranged for the editors and publishers of school books.

3. Consumer Education

49. The first issue of Kuluttajatietoa (Consumer Information) published during the period under review was edited for the purpose of serving as complementary material for teachers in the lower forms. The National Board of General Education, the National Board of Vocational Education and the National Board of Trade and Consumer Interests have co-operated in giving consumer education in schools. The National Board of Vocational Education has presented its teaching plan for the vocational training of teachers.

4. Redress and Complaints facilities

50. In 1983 the Consumer Complaints Board registered a total of 3 864 written complaints from consumers. The Board issued 1 456 recommendatory decisions. 1 040 cases were dropped without the Board's recommendation.

51. In 1983 the Consumer Ombudsman received 972 new notifications of marketing or contract terms. 764 cases were taken up for consideration. At the end of the year the number of pending cases was 1 295. Eight cases were referred to the Market Court.

III. RELATIONS BETWEEN CONSUMER POLICY AND OTHER ASPECTS OF GOVERNMENTAL POLICY

1. Government programme

52.   In his government programme issued in spring 1983 Prime Minister Sorsa considered it vitally important to reduce the rate of inflation in Finland. According to the programme inflation would be cut down by means of the Government's tariff and price policy. The Government promised to take measures to limit and do away with such measures as are responsible for maintaining an inflationary pressure. In its programme the Government also promised to make competition policy more effective. Although these measures are primarily motivated by the necessity to protect international competitiveness, the consumers would also benefit from a reduction in the rate of inflation. A considerable slow-down is expected to take place in 1984.

2. Price developments

53.   Consumer prices increased in Finland in 1983 by 8.4 per cent on an annual basis. This is 1 per cent less than in 1982. At the end of the year the rate of increase was roughly the same as at the beginning of the year. The rate of inflation was in Finland in 1983 3 per cent higher than in the OECD countries on an average. Of the factors contributing to the high rate of inflation in Finland can be mentioned the devaluation of the Finnish mark in autumn 1982 and the increase in sales tax by 2 per cent from the beginning of June 1983.

3. Price and competition policy

54.   At the end of 1982 the enlarged session of the National Board of Trade and Consumer Interests accepted a memorandum concerning the development of price and competition controls. According to the memorandum, efficient competition will guarantee a reasonable consumer price level. If price-fixing is too rigid and schematic, competition will easily lose most of its price-regulating power. For this reason the National Board of Trade and Consumer Interests has decided to reduce the extent of price controls in those branches where a reasonable price level is determined by the market powers. The personal resources thus freed from price controls will be transferred to economic research work. In addition to satisfying the need for information for administrative purposes by various government authorities, the national Board of Trade and Consumer Interests seeks to take advantage of the research results by increasing, among other things, the price consciousness of the consumers.

FRANCE

I. DEVELOPMENTS IN SUBSTANTIVE LAW AND WORK OF THE COMMISSIONS

A. A MAJOR LEGISLATIVE DEVELOPMENT: THE ACT OF 21ST JULY 1983 ON CONSUMER SAFETY

1. Principles of the 1983 Act

These principles are three in number and concern:

-- The general obligation concerning safety of products;

-- General prevention of risks;

-- Dialogue with the social partners on consumer risks

a) General obligation concerning safety of products

1.   This is the subject of Section 1 of the Act, which states: "Products and services shall under normal conditions of use and other conditions reasonably foreseeable by the trader meet legitimate expectations as to safety and not be prejudicial to health."

b) General prevention of risks

2.   This is the second basic principle of the Act. It is clearly set out, notably in Section 20, which adds a provision to the Act of 1st August 1905 on cheating in commercial transactions and adulteration. This new provision (Section 11.4) stipulates that "from the first placing on the market, products must comply with the health and safety, fair trading and consumer protection regulations. The person responsible for first placing an article on the market shall therefore be obliged to check that it complies with the regulations in force. At the request of the officials qualified to implement the present Act, he shall provide proof that the requisite checks and inspection have been carried out."

3.   This preventive aspect of the Act is echoed in Section 7, which provides various means whereby the Government can induce manufacturers,

55

importers, distributors and suppliers of services to bring the goods and services sold to consumers into line with the safety rules.

4.   The Act also enables the Government (Section 2) to introduce regulations laying down the circumstances in which manufacture, import, export, sale, ... labelling, packaging and presentation and method of use ... are prohibited or regulated with a view to consumer safety.

5.   The same section makes it possible to withdraw suspect products from the market and destroy them "when this is the only way of removing the danger".

c) Dialogue with the social partners

6.   It has been clearly stated that the safety legislation must not be a means of expressing suspicion of manufacturers and traders in general, but essentially an inducement to make them appreciate a concern of society -- safety. The Act therefore provides that all parties concerned may both explain and defend their point of view when specific cases come up before a body which should play a prime role in this respect: the Consumer Safety Commission. A Decree supplementing the Act specifies that the manufacturers or traders directly implicated in a product safety case must be given a hearing by this body.

2. Operative part of the Act of 21st July 1983

7.   This comprises two series of provisions: the first give various authorities (government, legal, public offices) extensive powers of intervention either to prevent or to put a stop to a consumer risk. The others set up a body which is original in more than one respect and has a wide range of duties: the Commission de la Sécurité des Consommateurs (C.S.C.) (Consumer Safety Commission).

a) Extensive powers of intervention

8.   Before we describe the main features of the provisions now applying in France, it must be remembered that the Government had already been given certain powers by the Act of 10th January 1978, albeit far from as comprehensive as the 1983 provisions.

9.   These powers of intervention are invested either in the Government, a public office or a judge.

i) Government powers

10.   The Government has extensive regulatory power enabling it to intervene in the various possible cases arising. It may use a permanent intervention procedure which, as mentioned earlier, allows it to take preventive measures by decree to regulate a given type of product. This procedure provides in particular for the possibility of withdrawing a product from the market ("recall" procedure), which is new compared with previous legislation. It must be noted that this regulatory power cannot be used against goods or

services covered by special legislation or Community regulations whose purpose is to protect consumer health and safety. However, this bar on intervention is waived in an emergency.

11.   The emergency procedure operates in the event of serious or immediate danger. The 1983 Act provides for emergency procedure which does not offer the same guarantees as the permanent procedure but on the other hand consists of temporary measures only. It enables the Minister for Consumer Affairs and other ministers concerned (Section 3), simply by a departmental order and without previously consulting the Consumer Safety Commission, to take the measures which would normally follow the longer decree procedure and consultation of the Conseil d'Etat. These departmental orders are valid for one year only. The Ministers must at once give a hearing to the traders concerned and, at the latest, within two weeks of a decision suspending marketing.

12.   It should be noted that emergency measures may even be taken for products subject to special domestic or Community legislation. It is the serious or immediate danger which justifies derogations.

13.   The injunction procedure caps the permanent intervention and emergency procedures (Section 7). The State Secretary responsible for Consumer Affairs may caution traders and charge them to bring goods or services into line with the safety rules or else submit these goods or services for inspection by an authorised agency chosen from a list which will be published by decree.

ii) Powers of public offices

14.   The intended aim is to give designated public officials the power to intervene during production, manufacture or processing at whatever place -- trade premises, factory or farm. The main officials concerned belong of course to the Directorate for Consumer Affairs and for the Prevention of Fraud (DCRF).

15.   Section 5 of the Act defines the powers of these officials.

16.   Another possibility granted public officials by the 1983 Act is the power of "consignment" for not more than two weeks, under legal control. For all their operations inspectors are empowered to order the communication and if necessary the seizure of any documents. They may also demand to see any vouchers proving that the compulsory pre-marketing inspection has been carried out by the trader.

17.   Among the authorities invested with new powers, mention should also be made of the important role devolving on the "Commissaires de la République", who are both government representatives in the Departments and the hierarchical heads of the various public offices in those Departments (Section 6). The Commissaires may in particular take any emergency measures necessary in their district providing that they report to the State Secretary responsible for Consumer Affairs, who in turn takes a decision within two weeks. In the meantime, the Commissaires may order the consignment of the suspect goods.

iii) Powers of the Judge

18.   Section 11 also invests the Judge with special powers with respect to safety. When an action is brought before him, he may order that the sale of goods or services involved be temporarily suspended. Such orders must be implemented, even if notice of appeal has been given.

19.   In the event of a judgement on merits, the sanctions are varied, ranging from the circulation or broadcast of notices to the public to confiscation and destruction of the dangerous goods. Lastly, the legal authority may refer the matter to the Consumer Safety Commission at any point in the proceedings.

b) The Consumer Safety Commission (C.S.C.)

20.   Before describing the duties of the CSC and the role it is supposed to play, a word should be said about its composition, which underlines the importance of this Commission within the system.

i) Composition

21.   Under a Chairman appointed by the Council of Ministers the Commission is composed of senior magistrates from the "Conseil d'Etat" the "Cour de Cassation" (Supreme Court of Appeal), and the "Cour des Comptes" (State Audit Office), representatives of consumers and traders appointed on the proposal of the National Consumer Council, and representatives of the Assemblies of the Conseil Supérieur d'Hygiène (Supreme Council on Health), the Institut National pour la Santé et la Recherche Médicale (INSERM), (National Institute for Health and Medical Research), the National Testing Laboratory and the National Sickness Insurance Fund (CNAM).

ii) Powers

22.   The Commission is responsible for delivering opinions and proposing any measure which might improve the prevention of risks attaching to goods and services (Section 14). It also has the job of finding and filing information from all sources on consumer hazards.

23.   Matters may be referred to it by any natural person or corporate body, but it may make an ex-officio investigation, and the government or legal authority may also refer a case to it.

24.   It has wide powers of investigation but is, on the other hand, obliged to give a hearing to all the parties involved and especially the traders concerned.

25.   Its power of recommendation and the influence of the opinions it gives are strengthened by the fact that it makes an annual report on its activities (and opinions) to the President of the Republic and to Parliament.

26.   The Commission is thus half way between a jurisdictional institution and an autonomous administrative institution employing inspectorate officials who come under its sole authority for this purpose.

B. WORK OF THE COMMISSIONS

1. Commission on the revision of consumer law (CRDC)

27.   The mandate of the Commission on the revision of consumer law, which was set up by the Decree of 25th February 1982, is to review existing consumer law, looking for any gaps and determine how they should be filled.

28.   After its second year in operation, the Commission on the revision of consumer law has made an interim report to the Secretary of State for Consumer Affairs describing the work already carried out and making a number of proposals on the following seven points:

1.   Consumer organisations: the proposal is to recognise and develop the role of the consumer associations by clarifying the definition of these associations, and the criteria of their representativeness and the procedure for assessing their position in the light of these criteria.

2.   Consumer information: the report proposes measures to improve the information provided for consumers by traders and the consumer organisations.

3.   Conformity of goods and services: this chapter contains two kinds of provisions; the first are preventive and seek to remove from the market those goods or services which do not come up to consumers' legitimate expectations. The others concern compensation when goods or services actually supplied do not meet these expectations.

4.   Consumer safety: this chapter was useful for the drafting of the Consumer Safety Act of 21st July 1983 as well as for the creation and establishment of the Consumer Safety Commission.

5.   Pre-drafted contracts: in this chapter on the action taken to prevent the inclusion of improper clauses and on trader-consumer contractual relations, the Commission proposes that legislation set a framework for the negotiation of standard contracts between traders' and consumers' representative organisations, accompanied by a list of improper clauses.

6.   Collectively negotiated agreements: the Commission proposes, as a general rule, that a framework for contractual agreements between consumers' and traders' organisations be established at national or local level, specifying the means whereby the Government could extend such agreements.

7.   Settlement of disputes: apart from practical measures to facilitate access to the law, the Commission suggests a simplified procedure for the settlement of minor consumer disputes by the court regarded as the natural jurisdiction for this type of dispute, and the launching of group action by the consumer organisations themselves.

29.   The Commission on the revision of consumer law will wind up its work in 1984. During its last year, it will examine trading methods, consumer credit and price controls.

2. The Commission on improper clauses

30.   The Commission on improper clauses, set up by Act No. 78-23 of 10th January 1978, examines the standard agreements usually offered by traders to their non-trade contractors or to consumers with a view to seeking out any improper clauses.

31.   During its sixth year of operation, the Commission was asked to examine 29 cases. It issued three recommendations, concerning land passenger transport contracts, open air holiday accommodation contracts and contracts for the bulk supply of liquefied petroleum gas. It also considered a Bill on price indexing clauses in private housebuilding contracts. Lastly, it published an annual activity report commenting on the work done and containing proposals for the revision of legislation or regulations.

32.   In 1984, the Commission on improper clauses, whose members' 3-year mandate will be renewed, will examine multiple-risk house insurance contracts, motor vehicle sale contracts, hire-purchase agreements and the internal rules for the running of old people's homes.

3. The Commission on the settlement of disputes

33.   There is no lack of legislation and regulations on the protection of consumers' interests, but the isolated consumer who wishes to take legal proceedings to claim his rights comes up against many difficulties.

34.   The unsuitability of the simplified procedures and the non-existence of collective procedures are additional obstacles.

35.   These observations dominated the discussions of the working party set up in February 1983 by the State Secretariat for Consumer Affairs and the Ministry of Justice.

36.   Its conclusions took three main directions:

-- Prevention of disputes;

-- Improvement of the individual settlement of disputes;

-- Introduction of procedure for the collective settlement of disputes.

On the prevention of disputes

37.   Apart from the necessity to improve methods of informing and training consumers and the various intermediaries (public offices, associations), the Commission was wholly in favour of more agreements between traders and consumer associations. The signing of such agreements and the climate of consultation that this assumes should prevent many disputes or at least facilitate their settlement out of court.

On improvement of the individual settlement of disputes

38.   There are three main courses here:

-- Improved access to the law: the Commission proposes that a case be brought by lodging an application with the clerk of the court using a simplified form;

-- In addition, in introducing a single method of referral to the court, steps should be taken to encourage conciliation as well as the use of simplified settlement forms (injunction-to-pay type);

-- Reduction of proceedings costs, mainly by cutting down on lengthy and expensive expert appraisements.

C. INTRODUCTION OF COLLECTIVE ACTION PROCEDURE

39.   Group action, whereby a single procedure settles disputes between many plaintiffs and one and the same defendant seems particularly appropriate for the settlement of consumer disputes.

40.   The Commission agreed that there was an unsatisfied need regarding the difficulty of obtaining in law:

-- Either compensation for repetitive damage;

-- The withdrawal of certain goods or the cessation of certain practices;

-- Or the deletion of improper clauses.

41.   At present, an isolated consumer has difficulty in instituting such proceedings. Group action should therefore be taken, adopting a two-phase procedure:

1. Judgement in principle.

2. Grouping of individual cases and final settlement.

II. EFFORTS TO IMPROVE CONSUMER PROTECTION

A. STANDARDIZATION AS A MEANS TO ENSURE THE SAFETY OF INDUSTRIAL PRODUCTS

42.   As in 1982, an agreement signed with AFNOR and funded by the State Secretariat for Consumer Affairs enabled several standardization projects regarded as urgent by the consumer associations to be carried through, including:

-- The revision of standards NFD 60.001 and 60.002 on furniture terminology;

-- Study of the feasibility of an "Eiderdowns and quilts" standard which, in addition to the terminology, would take account of mechanical, physical and especially heat-retention characteristics;

-- Revision of toy standards made necessary by constant changes in these articles and the obligation to take account of new versions of the corresponding European standards;

-- Standardization of various child-care articles: carrycots, changing tables, dummies;

-- A study on "Tricks and pratical jokes" articles not covered by the "toys" standards and responsible for many corporal accidents.

43. Similarly, an agreement was signed in 1983 with the National Testing Laboratory on the following matters:

-- Participation in funding an Ergonomics Laboratory to study user attitudes to the various consumer goods;

-- Funding for the technical assistance work required to complete the above-mentioned standardization projects;

-- Studies and laboratory tests on articles sampled by the DCRF during checks on the conformity of marketed goods with the regulations in force.

B. SINGLE MEASURES AND ACTION BY STAGES

44. The following measures should be mentioned in this context:

1) Health and safety measures

-- With the rapid development of collective catering, buying and settling of used frying oil or fat has considerably increased. The trade organisations concerned have been reminded that these waste products may be recovered only for use in soap-making or possibly by the animal feedingstuffs industry. Quality standards must be envisaged in the latter case. This problem is now under study at the Technical Centre in consultation with the department concerned.

-- Materials in contact with foodstuffs: sampling of plates and dishes or cooking pots for migration of lead and cadmium to ensure that this only rarely exceeded the regulation limits.

2) Accident prevention, economic protection of consumers and users

Foodstuffs

-- Withdrawal of imported foodstuffs (sandwich spreads, tinned mushrooms) liable to cause food poisoning.

Children's articles

-- Withdrawal of certain main imported toys (make-up kits, toy guns, soft toys) not conforming with the safety standards.

Industrial goods

-- Withdrawal of motorcyclists' safety helmets and of grinding wheels not conforming with the safety standards and of real danger to the user.

3) Imported products controls

Seafood: statistical and quality control (hygiene, prohibited additives) with destruction of consignments found unfit for human consumption.

Animal feedingstuffs: permanent monitoring of raw materials as soon as unshipped.

Other foodstuffs: control of trade description, packing and presentation, and quality of pork butchers' produce, cheese, olive oil, margarine, beer, eggs and egg-based products.

C. PROSPECTS FOR THE PROGRESS OF COMMUNITY WORK

45.   On 12th December 1983, the EEC Council of Ministers met for the first time to discuss consumer protection. After a statement by the Commission of the European Communities, the Council of Ministers first reviewed developments in consumer policy at European level and then turned to various proposals for texts on:

-- Misleading advertising;

-- Doorstep sales;

-- Product liability.

46.   The Council successfully concluded this first meeting by approving a proposal for a Decision introducing a system for the rapid exchange of information on dangers arising from the use of consumer products. This system will operate between the Member States of the European Community to inform them of any serious and immediate danger arising from products, and to give consumers effective protection by ensuring that a dangerous product withdrawn from the market of one Member State is not sold in another Member State.

III. ENCOURAGEMENT OF CONSUMER CONSULTATION

47.   Recognition of the consumer organisations as the partners of the authorities and traders is an essential feature of the action by the State Secretariat for Consumer Affairs division of the Ministry of the Economy, Finance and the Budget.

A. THE NATIONAL CONSUMER COUNCIL

48.   1983 saw the creation, by Decree of 12th July 1983, of the National Consumer Council, composed of representatives of consumers and users and representatives of traders. It took over from a Committee which had no traders' representatives.

49.   This new Council has the double responsibility for co-operation and consultation:

-- It provides the opportunity for co-operation between the representatives of consumers, traders and the Government;

-- It is an advisory body which the Government can consult on its major consumer and user policy orientations.

50.   This reorganisation complements that of the National Consumer Institute carried out by decree in January 1983.

51.   It is within this framework that the Directorate for Consumer Affairs and the Prevention of Fraud has continued its support for the consumer organisations and given them aid (especially financial) to help associations to develop at the different levels. The associations department is specifically responsible for these matters at the Directorate's central offices.

52.   A special training effort has been made on behalf of young consumers.

53.   In practical terms, this initiative has taken shape in the organisation of joint sessions for teachers, the documentary services of the Ministry of Education, consumer organisations, parents' associations and other Ministry of Education services.

54.   The State Secretariat for Consumer Affairs has joined the Ministry of Education in observing the experiments carried out by a number of pilot schools on consumer education and these have proved sufficiently positive for their extension to be considered already in 1984.

55.   The 1983 new school year was also the occasion for collaboration between the various partners concerned, when some parents' associations and consumer organisations undertook a price-watching campaign on school equipment.

56.   In higher education, the University of Haute Alsace has introduced courses in the consumer professions with the help of the State Secretariat for Consumer Affairs with a view to putting consumer affairs experts on the labour

market. The courses have a multidisciplinary approach unique in France and are at postgraduate level, sanctioned by a university diploma.

57.   In association with the Commission of the European Communities (which has been conducting pilot training activities in young consumer education since 1970), the State Secretariat for Consumer Affairs has helped to set up and develop a training course for teachers at the Auteuil Teacher Training College.

58.   In 1983, total grants made to encourage intermittent activities by consumer organisations and other associations to educate the young consumer increased from FF 690 000 to FF 1 290 000, or a rise of 87 per cent over 1982.

B. THE INTERMINISTERIAL COMMITTEE ON CONSUMER AFFAIRS

59.   Section 1 of the Decree of 23rd June 1983 set up an Interministerial Committee on Consumer Affairs in the Prime Minister's Office to consider interministerial proposals for action made on behalf of consumers and users by the Minister for Consumer Affairs. It can also examine Bills or Decrees having the same objective at this Minister's request.

60.   The Interministerial Committee is chaired by the Prime Minister or, in his absence, by the Minister or the Secretary of State for Consumer Affairs, and brings together at least twice a year those Ministers represented in the Interministerial Group on Consumer Affairs who are concerned by the meeting's Agenda.

I. INSTITUTIONAL DEVELOPMENTS IN THE FIELD OF CONSUMER POLICY

1.   In 1983, no special organisational or institutional changes of special relevance to consumers were recorded. In spite of the unfavourable budget situation, the Federal Government and the 11 Laender Governments made available in 1983 approximately DM 60.1 million (1982: roughly DM 58.9 million) for consumer information, consumer advisory services and the representation of consumer interests. Some DM 40.8 million (1982: about DM 40 million) of this total were accounted for by the Federal Government. This amount must be increased by other spending to the benefit of consumers, for instance information material of relevance to consumers, which the Federal Government publishes within the framework of its public relations activities, or spending on the promotion of consumer research.

II. REGULATORY OR OTHER ACTION CONCERNING CONSUMER PROTECTION, INFORMATION AND EDUCATION, AND MEANS OF REDRESS

1.   Consumer protection

    a) Physical protection (product safety)

    -- Veterinary medicines

2.   The first law to amend the Veterinary Medicine Law was promulgated in the Federal Gazette on 23rd February 1983. This law constitutes a fundamental improvement in the protection of consumers' health against residues of harmful substances in foodstuffs.

    -- Cosmetics

3.   The protection of consumers against harmful substances in cosmetics has been regulated by the 1974 Law on Foodstuffs and Goods in Daily Use and by the 1977 Cosmetics Regulations. By amending the Cosmetics Regulations, in the year under review, etidronic acid and its salts were admitted for use in the production of certain finished cosmetic products up to a specific maximum concentration. Previously, the drug regulations had subjected this, when used in medicine, to a prescription requirement. This explains why its use in cosmetics required formal permission.

-- Act on Plant Protection Agents

4.   The Federal Government submitted to the legislative bodies a draft bill on new plant protection agents. The new regulations are to adapt the present legal bases of plant protection to the latest standards of science and practice; especially, the trade and application provisions for plant protection agents are to be expanded and intensified to reduce the risks involved in plant protection.

-- Maximum Amounts of Plant Protection Agents Regulation

5.   The first Regulation on Maximum Amounts of Plant Protection Agents was submitted to the Bundesrat in December 1983. The maximum amounts provided for therein comply with the latest standards of science and technology. They take into account the need to protect human health. The values have been dimensioned so as to enable producers and processors to comply with them.

-- Regulation on Sewage Sludge

6.   The Sewage Sludge Regulation came into effect on 1st April 1983. The values limiting the contents of heavy metals in sewage sludge have been dimensioned so as to keep the impact on foodstuffs produced on sewage sludge-treated areas as low as possible.

-- Research projects, studies

7.   At the request of the Federal Ministry of Labour and the Social Order, the Federal Institute for Industrial Medicine and the Prevention of Industrial Accidents carried out projects and/or commissioned studies on the following subjects:

-- Determination of footwear sole gliding properties on floor coverings;

-- Safety criteria for incorporation in a new IAS ski bindings regulation to be prepared;

-- Structure of safety education and accident prevention films for display in schools, business, private houses, leisure time occupations and road traffic;

-- Safety at home and in leisure time occupations by properly designed instruments, tools and equipment safe to handle;

-- Collection of examples of safely designed living space and public facilities for the handicapped;

-- Analysis of accidents suffered at home and in leisure time occupations;

-- Data collected by sickness funds on accidents having occurred at home and in leisure time occupations;

-- Analysis of fatal accidents involving electricity;

-- Change of function over time of electrical safety switches for small currents.

8.   Federal Research Institutions focusing their activities on nutrition
have recently increased the physiological and toxicological examination of
food components and contaminants. In this context they have concentrated
mainly on mycotoxins.

9.   As suggested by more recent scientific analyses, a clear improvement
has been recorded for residues of plant protection agents. Only in a small
number of cases imported fruits and vegetables have been found to exceed
limiting values. Moreover, whole-diet studies covering roughly 50 substances
support the thesis that it would in no case be justified to say that undesired
substances have been posing a threat to human health. The real intake of undesired substances has partly been lower than hitherto assumed.

-- Miscellaneous

10.   The efforts of many years to clarify complex questions of "alternative
farming" have been continued with the aim of identifying pros and cons and
making results available to farmers and consumers. Special attention has
furthermore been paid to nitrates in water and foodstuffs as well as to con-
trolling the pollution of the soil as a basis of food production.

b) Protection of economic interests

-- Wine Regulations

11.   The Fifth Regulation of 4th August 1983, to amend the Wine Regulations
limits the permissible foreign elements in origin, variety and vintage labelling. The introduction of a new scheme is aimed at improving quality assessment. Moreover, the Regulation encompasses naming rules.

-- Poultry Grade Regulations

12.   The Grade Regulations for Poultry of April 1983, introducing the Grade
"extra" for heavy-weight poultry represent the first attempt to take into
account also invisible quality characteristics (e.g. better meat quality and
improved tastiness of heavy-weight fattened poultry).

-- German Food Manual

13.   The German Food Manual represents a collection of guidelines describing
production, quality and other food properties of importance to trade in foodstuffs. The German Food Manual Commission, in the reporting year, adopted new
guidelines on "cooked salted meat products", "minced meat", "fricassee",
"ragout" and "shish kebab" and revised the section on "ginger bread cookies"
within the framework of the guidelines on non-perishable bread and
confectionary.

2.   Consumer information

a) Labelling

14.   One of the major deadlines of the Ordinance on Food Labelling having

68

entered into force on 31st December 1981, expired on 26th December 1983. Prior to 31st December 1981, producers had the choice of labelling packaged foodstuffs either under the old or under the new provisions. Apart from various exceptions applicable especially to foodstuffs of a minimum durability of over 18 months, all prepacked foodstuff labels must carry the prescribed data, i.e. minimum durability and ingredients.

b) Comparative testing

15.   Comparative testing makes it easier for consumers to choose thus helping them to make ends meet. The Consumer Goods Testing Foundation, which will celebrate its 20th birthday this year, and its public relations work is indispensable for what happens in this country's markets. Wide sections of the German population have adopted the Foundation's work to guide their daily buying decisions. Not less important is the impact of comparative testing on producers and distributors.

16.   It is not least the fact that the Foundation is no pressure group that gives it its special credibility, but its status as an independent foundation on whose advisory board representatives of consumers and industry as well as independent experts sit in an advisory capacity.

17.   One focus in the Foundation's comparative testing is the classical consumer goods field with the energy sector having a fair share in it. Another focus is on services, and the Foundation looks into not only private, but also public services.

18.   The objects to be chosen for testing, the testing and assessment criteria are laid down in detail for each testing project. Product safety plays a special role in this context. But the Foundation takes good care also of other trends: the environmental impact of products is increasingly being taken into consideration in comparative testing. Since many products have meanwhile been advertised as low-polluting products, the Foundation verifies also the truth of such advertising slogans.

19.   The Comparative Goods Testing Foundation also tries to attract the attention of young consumers. Therefore, it organised again in 1983 a nation-wide competition entitled "testing by young persons"; this was the fourth competition of its kind. Roughly 600 young persons aged between 14 and 20 participated in this competition with about 152 tests in all. Twenty prizes have been awarded by an independent jury.

20.   The echo the Foundation's work has with the general public is also reflected by the edition of the Test Journal. The average number of copies printed per month in 1983 was 730 000. Although the number of copies has declined, it is nevertheless gratifying to note that the Journal has many readers also in economically difficult times.

c) Advisory services

21.   In 1983 as well, a number of private consumer organisations providing information and advisory services for consumers continued to receive public financial assistance. By way of example, the 11 Land consumer centres should be mentioned that -- with their more than 150 local advisory bureaux

-- represent important places for consumers seeking advice. The great variety of advisory services -- the range of services on offer encompasses purchasing advice including assistance with complaints as well as budgetary, nutritional and energy counselling -- was again used by numerous consumers in 1983.

22. In the field of education and information on nutrition questions the consumer centres -- most of them located in large and medium-sized cities -- and the rural home economics official advisory services of the Laender -- mainly located in rural districts -- the Evaluation and Information Service for Food, Agriculture and Forestry (AID) have been co-operating closely. Activities were mainly focused on information on questions of nutrition, on food markets and prices as well as -- owing to increased consumer demand -- on quality problems and the contamination of foodstuffs by harmful substances. In 1983, the Federal Minister of Food, Agriculture and Forestry spent over DM 7 million on nutritional information and education.

23. In order to mention one more example, the Federal Ministry of Labour and the Social Order supported the non-profit-making "Safety-At-Home Institution" with an amount of DM 120 000. It is this Institution's objective to inform the population on potential dangers and scope for protection against accidents at home and in leisure-time occupations and to sharpen its awareness with regard to safety risks.

d) Mass media

24. For many years on end, the media have done valuable consumer information work. This is often done in co-operation with consumer organisations and the Comparative Goods Testing Foundation.

25. The so-called new media, too, especially videotex, are means to offer consumers information unrelated to producers. Consumer organisations and the Comparative Goods Testing Foundation used this medium in 1983 by offering information of their own. The German PTT organised a number of PR measures on the occasion of the inauguration of videotex on 1st September 1983. Other PR measures have been designed to provide large sections of the population with more detailed information on cable TV connection -- the system and its advantages.

26. With a view to promoting TV and cinema consumer information films, the Association of Consumers (AgV) held its seventh international consumer information film competition in Berlin in January 1983.

e) Other advisory activities

27. The Federal Government's Press and Information Office re-edited and published at the end of 1983 its "Consumer Guideline". In over 200 pages, readers obtain information, suggestions and advice on daily consumer problems. The demand for this publication has been extraordinarily brisk; the re-edited 400 000 copies were sold out in a very short time. Other information material has been made available by other departments and consumer organisations.

28. Between August and November 1983, the information drive "congested

telephone lines during low-rate hours", which had been started a year earlier, was continued with a new series of advertisements in illustrated and news magazines. These advertisements are meant to inform telephone subscribers that reduced rates are charged not only between 6 p.m. and 8 p.m. on working days but throughout the night and at weekends. This drive's long-term aim is to change telephone habits and to help cut off the traffic peak on working days between 6 p.m. and 8 p.m.

3. Consumer education

29.   Education as critical consumers must start very early. Therefore, consumer education was included in school syllabuses many years ago already. Adult education also focuses on this subject. Wherever possible, consumer organisations also help in this field.

4. Complaints

30.   Consumers, before taking disputes to attorneys and courts, have got a possibility in many cases to submit such disputes to arbitration or mediation; this is possible, for instance, in the automobile repair, textiles dry cleaning, shoe repair, radio and TV repair, automobile towing and the building industries as well as in medicine. Moreover, all chambers of commerce and industry as well as craft chambers are prepared to pursue consumer complaints; many of these chambers, including craft chambers, have set up special arbitration and mediation boards. The nature, working methods and ways to make use of the services of such boards are different. However, it would be fair to say that in the period under review they were able to help a large number of consumers. Consumers have widely taken advantage of the services offered by consumer centres and their advisory bureaux which also help them to enforce their claims outside the court system. This type of assistance has been a major focus in their activities for many years already.

III. CONSUMER AND OTHER POLICY AREAS

-- Energy conservation

31.   The Comparative Goods Testing Foundation and the Association of Consumers continued their special advisory and information activities on energy conservation making available to this end budgetary funds worth roughly DM 5.8 million in 1983.

32.   Within the framework of these activities, the Comparative Goods Testing Foundation again commissioned a number of additional comparative tests, supplemented by reports containing information on how to save energy. The test results and reports were published on special pages of the monthly "test" magazine and were also disseminated by TV spots inter alia.

33.   The Association of Consumers continued to secure the services of a

large number of energy experts (e.g. engineers and architects) to give advice on special problems free of charge to interested consumers at the local advisory bureaux of consumer centres. Such experts can be consulted at 140 advisory bureaux. This advisory service has been used by many consumers, in particular, by owners of private houses and flats and -- increasingly also by tenants. Advice has been asked for mainly on questions concerning the thermal insulation of buildings construction-related physics, heating plant technology as well as issues concerning government promotion of energy conservation as well as heating cost billing in conformity with actual consumption.

34.   For advice on energy conservation mainly in less densely populated areas, the Association of Consumers operated a mobile unit especially equipped for energy conservation counselling in the whole of 1983. This project, started in 1982, has proved to be successful and will therefore be continued.

-- Environment

35.   In the Federal Republic of Germany, the "Environmental Symbol" may be awarded to ecologically unobjectionable products. This subject was amply discussed in last year's report. The Environmental Symbol is very popular. At present, applications for its award may be filed in 26 different lines of production as distinct from 21 last year. Products topping the list of producers entitled to use the Environmental Symbol are low-polluting pulverised oil burners, lacquers and salt-free skid-prevention agents.

36.   The Environmental Symbol is also used by many importers.

37.   Environmental issues relevant to consumers deserve special importance also in the work of private consumer organisations. In 1983, there were a number of publications and seminars focusing on environmental subjects.

-- Matches monopoly

38.   The act to abolish the matches monopoly signed on 27th August 1982, entered into force on 16th January 1983, thus abolishing the matches monopoly. This means that there is no longer any state control over match prices.

-- Automobile insurance premiums

39.   It has been intended in the field of motor insurance to release motor insurance premiums from governmental control after an appropriate transitional period. The date envisaged for such deregulation is 1st April 1985. This measure represents another step toward liberalisation of motor insurance and implementation of market economy principles.

-- Deregulation

40.   Within the efforts made to improve economic growth prospects and to help reduce unemployment, it is particularly important in the Federal Government's opinion to free industry and private individuals from unnecessary governmental control narrowing their scope for action. Deregulation is not only an ongoing task for public authorities, but it also requires citizens to rethink and rely less on public benefits by making provision for themselves instead.

I. INSTITUTIONAL DEVELOPMENTS

1.   No major institutional development occurred in 1983.

2.   Responsible for the protection and information of Greek Consumers is the Ministry of Commerce mainly through the Consumers' Protection and Information Service. However a number of other Ministries (Ministry of Agriculture, of Health, of Transport and Communications, of Maritime Transport, of Physical Housing and Environment) also serve the interests of the consumers.

II. NEW REGULATIONS OR MODIFICATONS TO EXISTING LAWS

1. Consumer protection

a) Physical protection

i) Transport

3.   The Ministry of Transport and Communications decided to continue the partial replacement of the existing buses, trolley-buses and subway carriages with new ones in order to increase the safety of passengers.

4.   The Civil Aviation Service, responsible for air safety, took measures to improve the safety of flights and the smooth an rapid flow of air traffic.

5.   The Greek Organisation of Railways in order to improve passengers' safety installed a new telecommunications system.

ii) Agriculture

6.   The Ministry of Agriculture responsible also for the qualitative and technological inspection of farm produce processing factories:

    -- Organised a 38-day seminar to train 21 agriculturists in matters concerning standardization and quality control of processed farm products;

-- Prepared a decree standardizing the quality of canned peaches;

-- Issued a number of circulars concerning quality control of peach-nectar;

-- Carried out a number of veterinary inspections of meat and vegetables throughout the country.

b) Protection of economic interests

i) Transport and communications

7.   The Ministry of Transport and Communications with the general framework of established Governmental Policy decided to keep the public transportation cost relatively low. So buses, trolley-buses and subway are used free of charge from 05:00 to 08:00 hrs. and the price of the monthly transport card (which gives access to all civil means of transport for an unlimited number of routes) remained at Dr 700. The prices of tickets of inter-city coaches was also kept at relatively low levels.

8.   A survey was undertaken by the Ministry of Transport for the improvement of the air traffic in the greater Athens area. Questionnaires were distributed to the passengers of the Civil Transport Corporation and further information was collected by personal contact with passengers. Moreover the re-orientation and extension of existing routes and the initiation of new ones especially in the Athens area are under study. For the information of the public as to these changes, informative leaflets were issued and distributed.

9.   To improve the service of taxi passengers and tourists the price lists hanging in the taxi cabs are now to be written in both Greek and English; moreover, informative boards were placed in airports, ports, railway stations and bus terminals, with useful information about taxi fares, etc.

10.   The Greek Organisation of Railways issued cheaper tickets for special categories of passengers (youngsters, elderly people, students). Moreover new booking-offices started to operate for the better service of the public.

11.   The Greek Post Office initiated a new Coding Systm and new post offices started to operate for the better service of the public. After 2 1/2 years freeze, postage cost was raised by an average of 28.3 per cent for the domestic mail and 37 per cent for the international mail.

12.   The Greek National Organisation of Telecommunications continued renewing their infrastructure (new telephone exchanges, new networks, etc.) in order to improve the quality of services offered to the public.

ii) Tourism

13.   The Greek National Tourism Organisation continued their efforts to improve the quality of services offered by tourist enterprises. A new law is under study which would provide for better protection of tourists from abusive practices from travel agents.

iii) Ministry of Commerce

14.   The Consumers' Protection and Information Service which is supervised directly by the Undersecretary of Commerce continued its activities throughout 1983. Namely:

-- It handled complaints made by consumers;

-- Intervened informally in disputes between merchants and consumers, so that lengthy and expensive court procedures would be avoided;

-- Collaborated with the market police in matters concerning price and quality control;

-- Analysed consumer complaints and when serious problems were detected they were worked out with other Ministries;

-- Prepared a law concerning misleading and unfair advertising;

-- Helped with the setting up of the National Consumers' Council which is an advisory agency in which are represented a number of consumers' organisations, labour unions and women's associations.

15.   The Directorate of Weights and Measures carried out throughout 1983 their annual control of weights and measures used in commercial transactions. Moreover:

i) A Presidential decree (No. 447/83) on automatic check weighing and weight grading machines was issued;

ii) A Presidential decree (No. 515/83) on units of measurement was issued;

iii) Market ordinance (28/83) on the accuracy of gas-meters of gas-filling stations was issued;

iv) Circular F3/1779/83 on the inspection of tank-trucks carrying diesel-oil was issued.

16.   The Directorate of Technological Protection of Consumption issued a number of ordinances.

More specifically:

i) Market ordinance (4/83) on unit pricing;

ii) Market ordinance (23/83) on date coding of instant drinks;

iii) Market ordinance (31/83) on the safety band for packed food-products;

iv) Market ordinance (38/83) which bans the sale of oils and greases by door-to-door salesmen;

v) Market ordinance (39/83) which makes it obligatory for all industrial products to be accompanied by prospectuses in Greek;

vi) Market ordinance (52/83) which makes it obligatory for all imported products to be labelled in Greek;

vii) Market ordinance (55/83) on the specification of the weight of
meat and fish wrapping.

17.   The Directorate of Vegetable Products issued a number of market ordinances regulating the prices and distribution of certain products, among which
are: refined olive oil, cotton seed oil, soya-bean oil, retsina wine, tomatoes, peeled potatoes, bananas, flour, bread and fir trees.

2. Consumer information

18.   The Consumers' Protection and Information Service continued its activities in the field of information throughout 1983.

More specifically:

-- A number of articles were published in newspapers and magazines to
   inform the public on certain consumer products, price discounts,
   etc.;

-- Several informative leaflets were issued and distributed to the
   public.

3. Consumer education

19.   The Ministry of Agriculture organised meetings and seminars for the
farm population providing information on the purchases of durable and other
consumer goods.

20.   The Consumers' Protection and Information Service published a book
titled "You are a consumer. What do you know about it?", intended primarily
for use as a high-school text-book.

IRELAND

I. INSTITUTIONAL DEVELOPMENTS IN THE FIELD OF CONSUMER POLICY

Ombudsman

1.   The first Ombudsman was appointed in December, 1983 (under the Ombudsman Act, 1980) and took up office in January, 1984. The Ombudsman speaks and acts on behalf of the individual citizen. Basically, he examines the actions of public officials in their handling of cases on behalf of the citizen and seeks a satisfactory remedy in those instances where he finds that a citizen has a genuine grievance. The Ombudsman deals with day to day administrative decisions and actions rather than with the broad scheme of Government policy or national affairs. Certain areas, for example, security matters and military activity, are exempt from his scrutiny.

2.   Initially, his remit is confined to Government Departments and offices staffed by civil servants. However, the Government is empowered to extend his jurisdiction to other bodies such as local authorities and health boards. The general public response to the establishment of the Ombudsman's Office has been gratifying and has indicated that this has been seen as a significant step forward in the area of general relationships between the citizen and the bureaucracy.

Public Service Development

3.   A Cabinet Minister with full time responsibility for the public service was appointed for the first time in 1982. Since his appointment, the Minister for the Public Service has taken a number of initiatives to improve the image of the civil service and to provide a better service to the public. These include a requirement that all civil servants dealing with the public in person or by letter identify themselves (in the case of civil servants working in public offices this means the wearing of an identification badge); that staff who deal directly with the public, and their supervisors, receive special training; that the layout, furnishing and decoration of public offices be improved; and that official forms be simplified. The Minister has assigned responsibility for work in this whole area to a section of his Department and further measures to make it easier, friendlier and more pleasant for the public in their dealings with Government Departments can be expected in the course of 1984.

Reorganisation of the Postal and Telecommunications Sector

4. Under the Postal and Telecommunications Services Act, 1983 and with effect from 1st January 1984, authority to provide postal services was vested in An Post (The Post Office) and authority to provide telecommunications services was vested in Bord Telecom Eireann (The Irish Telecommunications Board).

5. The Postal and Telecommunications Services Act, 1983 provides for the establishment of a Users' Council for each company. The members of the Councils shall be appointed by the Minister for Communications.

6. The Councils shall consider any complaint or representation made to them by or on behalf of a user or a prospective user of the services provided by the companies. The Councils may also consider any matter, other than matters of internal management, related to such services which appear to them to warrant consideration. They may also advise the Minister for Communications or the companies on any matter relating to postal or telecommunications services on which the Minister or the companies seek their advice.

7. These statutory Councils will replace the single non-statutory Post Office Users' Council which was established in 1974.

II. REGULATORY OR OTHER ACTION CONCERNING CONSUMER PROTECTION, INFORMATION AND EDUCATION, AND MEANS OF REDRESS

1. Consumer protection

a) Physical protection (product safety)

8. The Minister for Industry and Energy (now Industry, Trade, Commerce and Tourism) made the following Orders during 1983:

    i) The Industrial Research and Standards (Section 44) (Electrical Plugs and Sockets) Order, 1983, prohibits the manufacture, assembly or sale of electrical plugs or socket-outlets unless they meet certain specified safety requirements. The Order came into force on 1st August 1983;

    ii) The Industrial Research and Standards (Section 44) (Children's Cots) Order, 1983, prohibits the manufacture, assembly or sale of children's cots unless they comply with Irish Standard 250:1981 which provides minimum safety requirements for children's cots of fixed side, drop side and folding drop side type, made of timber or metal. The Order came into force on 1st September 1983;

    iii) The Industrial Research and Standards (Section 44) (Babies Dummies) Order, 1983, prohibits the manufacture, assembly or sale of babies' dummies unless they comply with Irish Standard 248:1981 which specifies safety requirements for babies' dummies and the testing procedure to be used for checking these requirements. The Order came into force on 1st September 1983;

iv) The Industrial Research and Standards (Section 44) (Gas Ovens) Order, 1983, prohibits the manufacture, assembly or sale of a gas-operated oven or an appliance containing such an oven, which is not fitted with a device to prevent the issue of unignited gas, which could cause an explosion or fire on subsequent ignition. The Order came into force on 1st September 1983;

v) The Industrial Research and Standards (Section 44) (Toxicity of Pencils and Graphic Instruments) Order, 1983, prohibits the manufacture, assembly or sale of pencils and graphic instruments unless they comply with Irish Standard 253:1982, being the Irish Standard specification for toxicity of pencils and graphic instruments. The Order came into force on 1st February 1984;

vi) The Industrial Research and Standards (Section 44) (Resemblance to Food of Non-Food Products Used by Children) Order, 1983, ensures that non-food products intended for use by children shall not be marketed in a design that would make them attractive to small children to eat. The Order came into force on 1st February 1984.

9.   The Minister for Health and Social Welfare made the following Regulations in 1983:

i) The Health (Antioxidant in Food) (Amendment) Regulations, 1983, implement Council Directive 81/962/EEC and came into force on 1st April 1983;

ii) The European Communities (Food Additives) (Purity Criteria Verification) Regulations, 1983, which implement Council Directive No. 81/712/EEC, came into force on 1st May 1983;

iii) The European Communities (Cosmetic Products) Regulations, 1984, consolidate and update the law in Ireland in relation to cosmetic products and give statutory effect to recent Council Directives relating to such products. (Directives 76/768, 79/661, 80/1335, 82/147, 82/368, 82/434, 83/191, 83/341, 83/496, 83/514, 83/574.) The effect of the Regulations is to prohibit the placing on the market of cosmetic products which, under normal conditions of use, are liable to be injurious to health. The Regulations came into force on 18th January 1984.

10.   The Minister for Agriculture made the following Regulations in 1983:

i) The European Communities (Feedingstuffs) (Additives) (Amendment) Regulations, 1983, amend the European Communities (Feedingstuffs) (Additives) Regulations 1974 to 1982 so as to bring into force amendments made to Council Directive 70/524/EEC through Commission Directive 82/474/EEC. The Regulations came into force on 21st February 1983;

ii) The European Communities (Feedingstuffs) (Additives) (Amendment) (No. 2) Regulations, 1983, amend the European Communities (Feedingstuffs) (Additives) Regulations 1974 to 1983 so as to bring into force amendments made to Council Directive 70/524/EEC through Commission Directive 82/822/EEC. The Regulations came into force on 24th June 1983.

iii) The European Communities (Feedingstuffs) (Additives) (Amendment)
(No. 3) Regulations, 1983, amend the European Communities (Feed-
ingstuffs) (Additives) Regulations, 1974 to 1983 so as to bring
into force amendments made to Council Directive 70/524/EEC through
Commission Directive 83/266/EEC and Commission Directive 83/466/
EEC. The Regulations came into force on 15th November 1983.

The annexes to Council Directive 70/524/EEC lay down which additives may be
used in feedingstuffs for growth promotion or disease protection. The Annexes
are amended from time to time by Commission Directives. One of the principal
reasons for these controls is the protection of human health.

b) Protection of the consumers' economic interest

11.   The European Communities (Aerosol Dispensers and Prepacked Goods) Regulations, 1983, which were made by the Minister for Trade, Commerce and Tourism
(now Industry, Trade, Commerce and Tourism) ensure that products prepackaged
in the sizes/capacities laid down in Council Directive 80/232/EEC ("Range of
Sizes") are guaranteed access onto the Irish market. The Regulations also encourage a reduction in the number of product sizes on the market thereby faci-
litating easier price comparisons. The Regulations came into force on
13th June 1983.

12.   The following Regulations were made under the Transport (Tour Operators
and Travel Agents) Act, 1982:

      i) The Tour Operators (Licensing) Regulations, 1983;

     ii) The Travel Agents (Licensing) Regulations, 1983;

    iii) The Tour Operators and Travel Agents (Bonding) Regulations, 1983;

     iv) The Travellers' Protection Fund Regulations, 1983;

      v) The Transport (Tour Operators and Travel Agents) (Claims by Custo-
mers) Regulations, 1983 and

     vi) The Transport (Tour Operators and Travel Agents) Act, 1982 (Com-
mencement) Order, 1983.

The Regulations implement provisions of the 1982 Act covering viz. licensing,
bonding, establishment of the protection fund and claims by customers. The
Act and the Regulations came into force on 1st November 1983.

13.   The Postal and Telecommunications Services Act, 1983 imposes a statutory obligation on An Post (The Post Office) and Bord Telecom Eireann (The
Irish Telecommunications Board), from 1st January 1984, to meet all reasonable
demands for comprehensive and efficient national postal and telecommunications
services, respectively, insofar as the companies consider it reasonably prac-
ticable to do so. No such obligation applied to the national postal and telecommunications services before 1st January 1984.

14.   The national postal and telecommunications services have for many years
enjoyed statutory limitation of liability to users etc., including exemption

from the Sale of Goods and Supply of Services Act, 1980. However, Sections 64 and 88 of the 1983 Act narrow the limitation of liability somewhat (by excluding cases of injury and neglect). They also provide enabling power for the Minister for Industry, Trade, Commerce and Tourism to make an Order, after consultation with the Minister for Communications, to apply the 1980 Act to such extent as he may specify to postal services provided within the State by An Post and to telecommunications services provided within the State by Bord Telecom Eireann.

15.   Other provisions of the Act prohibit unauthorised interference with, or interception of, postal packets and telecommunications messages and disclosure of information so obtained. Considerably increased penalties are also provided for many other offences against bona fide users of the national postal and telecommunications services.

2. Consumer Information

a) Labelling

Compulsory labelling

16.   The European Communities (Seeds of Oil Plants and Fibre Plants) (Amendment) Regulations, 1983, require that seed which has been officially labelled is of the variety, etc., purported on the label and is of a high standard. The Regulations, which were made by the Minister for Agriculture, came into force on 20th June, 1983.

17.   The European Communities (Labelling, Presentation and Advertising of Foodstuffs) Regulations, 1982, which were made by the Minister for Trade, Commerce and Tourism (now Industry, Trade, Commerce and Tourism) implement Council Directive 79/112/EEC on Food Labelling. The Regulations came into force on 1st December 1983.

18.   The European Communities (Indication of Prices of Foodstuffs) Regulations, 1983, give effect to Council Directive 79/581/EEC and require, in broad terms, with certain specific and general exceptions, that

i) The selling price of all foodstuffs, and

ii) The unit price of foodstuffs prepackaged in variable quantities or sold loose unpackaged by weight or volume,

will have to be displayed. The Regulations which were made by the Minister for Trade, Commerce and Tourism (now Industry, Trade, Commerce and Tourism) will come into force on 1st June 1984.

19.   The European Communities (Jewellery) Regulations, 1984, which were made by the Minister for Industry, Trade, Commerce and Tourism give effect to a European Court judgement regarding the origin-marking of souvenir jewellery imported from other Member States of the European Community. The provisions of the existing Merchandise Marks (Origin-Marking) orders will no longer apply to relevant imports from EEC countries and certain associates. The Regulations came into force on 1st February 1984.

b) Comparative testing

20.   There is no Government sponsored comparative testing in Ireland.

c) Other information activities

21.   The Office of the Director of Consumer Affairs received approximately 13 000 complaints in 1983.   The Office in addition to investigating approximately 600 complaints dealing with false or misleading trade practices (its principal function) also provided complainants with information on consumer legislation and their rights as consumers.   The Office also publicised consumer legislation.

22.   The Consumers' Association of Ireland (an independent Association) continued to operate a telephone Advice and Information Service which dealt with enquiries and complaints from members of the public.   The service, which operates five days a week, is provided free of charge.

23.   The National Social Services Board (originally known as the National Social Services Council) was established by the Minister of Health and Social Welfare in 1971 to promote co-operation and co-ordination between local social service agencies and to provide information and advice particularly to voluntary organisations.   The Board continued to service a network of voluntary Community Information Centres throughout the State which provided information on, inter alia, consumer rights.   The Centres also on occasion interceded on behalf of consumers who felt they had a grievance with a seller of goods or services.

24.   The Health Education Bureau produced a revised and updated version of its "Book of the Child", containing information on infant feeding (among other things), in 1983.   A specific handbook of infant feeding was also produced by the Bureau in 1983 and recommended dietary allowances for the population (revised from the 1977 allowances) were distributed by the Bureau during the year.

25.   The Tourist Traffic Act, 1983 gave the Irish Tourist Board the power to require a range of information, which would be of benefit to consumers using holiday accommodation, to be displayed in registered accommodation premises. The Act came into force on 15th November 1983.

3. Consumer Education

26.   The process of introducing consumer education into school programmes continues and many disciplines now include modules relating to the purchase and use of materials, the environment and avoidance of pollution, the rights of citizens and the forms and methods of redressing difficult situations.

27.   The Minister for Education, who announced a four-year action plan for education in 1984, has set up a curriculum and examination board which has the specific task of reviewing curricula in both the primary and post-primary areas as well as examining the need for reform in examinations and assessment procedures.   It is thus expected that the board in time will lay greater stress on education for living, and will thus concern itself with the needs of a consumer society.   Existing curricular committees revising programmes in

second-level subjects, have received a submission from the Consumers' Association of Ireland and hope to incorporate some of these suggestions in their proposed new syllabus.

28.   Arrangements are being made to hold a week-end seminar on consumer education at which both the Director of Consumer Affairs and leading educators in the field of consumer education will lecture to a variety of teachers on the needs, aims and objectives of consumer education in school programmes.

III. GENERAL REMARKS

Major Inquiry into Electricity Prices

29.   The burden of electricity charges has been the subject of complaint for some considerable time and repeated calls have been made particularly from industry to reduce the burden in order to improve competitiveness. For this reason, the Government decided that a full review should be carried out which would test the validity of the criticism and form a new basis for future planning and decision-making in relation to the Electricity Supply Board's general development and its pricing structure. To carry out this review an Inquiry Group with representatives from an electricity utility, industry and Government Departments was set up in May, 1983. The report of the group is expected by mid-1984 (approximately).

I. INSTITUTIONAL DEVELOPMENTS IN THE FIELD OF CONSUMER POLICY

1.   The number of Local Consumer Centres which conduct activities concerning the handling of consumer complaints, consumer education, product testing and other activities, totalled 253 as of April 1983, 131 being prefectural and 122 municipal; an increase of seven over the preceding year. These centres contribute to the consumer policy of local administrations.

2.   Concerning the consumer administration budget, refer to the table at the end of this report.

II. REGULATORY OR OTHER ACTION CONCERNING CONSUMER PROTECTION, INFORMATION AND EDUCATION, AND MEANS OF REDRESS

1. Consumer Protection

a) Physical Protection (Product Safety)

3.   A "Good Laboratory Practice Standard for Safety Studies on Drugs" (GLP) was formulated in March 1982, and was fully implemented as of April 1983 in order to further increase the reliability of data on animal experiments and others, which must be submitted together with application for approval of a new drug.

4.   Furthermore, re-evaluation work on already-approved drugs is continuing in the light of the latest medical and pharmaceutical findings, and the 21st Advice on ethical drugs was submitted by the Pharmaceutical Affairs Council to the government in April 1983. As a result, 100 of the approved ethical drugs, including psychotropic and neutrotropic drugs, were adjudged to be useless and measures were taken to remove them from the market. Re-evaluation work on non-prescription drugs has been under way since 1978. In April 1983, in accordance with the re-evaluation standards formulated in August 1981 for antitussives and expectorants, the results of the re-evaluation conducted on 168 non-prescription drugs were made public.

5.   In order to ensure the safety of foods, food additives, apparatuses, container-packages, etc., the Ministry of Health and Welfare formulated

standards and took additional steps for those foods, food additives, equipment, container-packages, etc. which are considered to require regulation as a result of investigation and testing, based on the Food Sanitation Law.

6.   As for food products, the Code of Hygiene Practice was formulated for the manufacture and handling of perishable cakes in March 1983.

7.   As for chemically-synthesized food additives, 11 items, including silicon dioxide, were newly designated as food additives in August 1983, in view of the increased imports of foods, recent changes in the nation's food environment and other conditions.   The standards for specification and usage were established for those newly designated food additives.   Furthermore, in view of increased usage, investigations concerning natural food additives are being conducted to evaluate their safety.

8.   The conventional individual standards for plastic resin-made equipment, containers and packages for food were unified into the Guidelines for the Food Packaging and Containers in June 1983.   The industry of such plastic products was instructed to voluntarily use these guidelines as its standard.

9.   The Consumer Products Safety Association, established under the Consumer Product Safety Law, authorises manufacturers to carry the SG (safety good) mark on their products if the products in question are approved as "safe" by the Association.   Using insurance facilities, the Association further gives compensation to consumers for damage caused by defects in the SG-mark products.   In February 1984, an approval criterion was established for nursery drawers.   As a result, 64 products are now allowed to carry SG-marks on them.

10.   In May 1983, according to the "Law for the Control of Household Products Containing Harmful Substances", two substances, tetrachloroethylene and trichloroethylene were designated as harmful and regulation standards were formulated for household detergents and aerosol products containing them.   At present, 17 substances are designated as "harmful" under this law.

11.   Important measures to improve the safety of buildings include regulation of sites, structure and facilities under the Building Standard Law, and that of fire-fighting equipment and fire prevention management under the Fire Service Law.

12.   The Architects Law and the Building Standards Law were partially revised in May 1983 in order to strengthen the supervision over the registered architects and their offices and to extend the scope of buildings covered by the periodical reporting system, aimed at the prevention of illegal construction and the proper maintenance and preservation of buildings.

13.   As for fire prevention measures, in April 1983 theatres and department stores were included among the buildings to which the "System for Indicating Conformity with the Fire Prevention Standard" ("the pass" mark system) is applied on a countrywide basis, following inns and hotels, to which the pass mark system has already been applied.

14.   Financing through the Small Business Finance Corporation and other financing institutions was started in 1983 to promote the implementation of the pass mark system.   Moreover, the government instructed the prefectural authorities to improve and expand such financing system.

b) Protection of the Consumers' Economic Interest

15.   The Consumer Policy Committee of the Social Policy Council conducted research and deliberated on measures to prevent consumer problems that would arise from the diversification of consumer transactions, and to promote quick and fair solutions to such problems. In December 1983, the Committee prepared and made public a report entitled "Concerning the Improvement of Consumer Transactions Outside the Seller's Normal Selling Premises" based on the results of such research and deliberations.

16.   The registration system for visiting salespersons is being promoted as a voluntary system of door-to-door sales enterprises in order to improve the quality of salespersons. As of January 1984, about 600 000 salespersons were registered.

17.   In order to promote the rationalisation of mail order transactions, it was decided to form an industry association that would cover all the industrial sectors concerned. As a result, the Japan Mail Order Sale Association was founded in October 1983.

18.   The Study Group on Consumer Credit Industry, established by MITI in June 1982 in order to study ways and means of solving problems in the consumer credit industry, deliberated on and published in July 1983 a report containing comprehensive protection of consumers and other topics.

19.   After studying preventive measures for consumer disputes that occur frequently in view of the increase in credit sales, the Consumer Affairs Committee of the Industrial Structure Council prepared in February 1984 a report entitled "Concerning Measures to Secure the Interest of Purchasers in Credit Transactions" in which purchasers are allowed to exercise their right to refuse payment to the charge company. In response to the report, the Ministry of International Trade and Industry is now working on an amendment to the Credit Sale Law to be submitted in the forthcoming session of the Diet.

20.   The Working Party on Stipulation Problems, formed in the Credit Sale Council studied the stipulation problems, including the definition of the services provided by the All Japan Family Ceremonial Affairs Mutual Aid Associations. In September 1983, the Party submitted a report concerning the rationalisation of agreement stipulations.

21.   The Money-Lending Business Control and Regulation Laws were established in May 1983 and enforced in November of the same year. The two laws provide for registration prior to the opening of a money-lending business, issuance of instruments such as written statements, regulation of certain acts of collection and other operations, regulation of high interest rates, etc. in order to protect the interests of those who need to borrow funds.

22.   The Economic Planning Agency promoted consumer education concerning consumer loan problems through the Japan Consumer Information Center and notified the prefectural authorities in July 1983 that they should promote educational activities.

23.   The police, continuing from the previous year, designated November 1983 as "Enforcement Month to strengthen the regulation of unfair loan cases", and launched a nationwide crackdown on unfair moneylenders to protect consumers.

24.   The legislation regarding consignment and other measures of future transactions in foreign commodity markets, intended to prevent unfair practices in future transactions in overseas commodity exchanges, came into effect in January 1983. The government took such steps as on-the-spot inspections, the issuance of business suspension orders and the announcement of such orders in accordance with that law.

25.   In order to cope with consumer problems originating from overseas commodity transactions, the Ministry of International Trade and Industry reinforced the conventional consultation system, and the Ministry of Agriculture, Forestry and Fisheries started the "emergent telephone service for overseas commodity transactions".

26.   In order to expedite the settlement of complaints and disputes arising from transactions of housing lots and buildings, the Ministry of Construction formed an Examination Committee. In March 1983, the Committee proposed that the current complaint settlement organs be effectively utilised and that a comprehensive organisation be established to supplement the activities of the complaint handling organs.

27.   The police, continuing from last year, designated May 1983 as "Enforcement Month to strengthen the regulation on the vicious real estate case" and launched a nationwide crackdown on unfair real estate dealers to protect consumers.

28.   The Consumer Policy Committee of the Social Policy Council has been studying the proper reform of contract provisions used by individual industrial sectors for consumer transactions, and has researched and deliberated on the correct regulation of contract provisions in Japan. As part of the research and deliberations, in November 1983 the Committee made public an interim report describing the results of the study on the reform of the contract provisions used by three service businesses, i.e., freight transportation, hotels, and warehousing. Furthermore, the Committee studied the proper reform of contract provisions used in damage insurance and banking as well as researched and deliberated on the proper reform of contract provisions in Japan. The results of the study were made public in May 1984.

2. Consumer Information

    a) Labelling

29.   A voluntary standardization system called "JAS" (Japanese Agricultural Standards), and a compulsory quality labelling system are enforced under the Law Concerning the Standardization and Proper Labelling of Agricultural and Forestry Products. In 1983, four "JAS" standards, including one for fruit drinks, and the quality labelling standard for fruit drinks, were revised. As of February 1984, there were 409 "JAS" standards (including 331 for beverages and food-stuffs), and 39 compulsory quality labelling standards.

30.   The requirement to label the substance or category name had already been specified for 68 food additives in accordance with the Food Sanitation Law. In addition, in August 1983, 10 newly-designated food additives required labelling of the substance and six of these also required labelling of the category.

87

31.   Under the Industrial Standardization Law, the "JIS" (Japanese Industrial Standard) is formulated for clothing, electrical appliances and many
other consumer daily products in order to rationalise consumer living through
improvement of their quality. In 1983, the "JIS" standard for shoe sizes was
formulated and those for erasersand other products were revised. Furthermore,
electronic jars and other products were added to those products requiring
labelling in accordance with the JIS-mark labelling system.

32.   In order to promote the wider use of "JIS", PR Pamphlets were distributed to consumer groups and questioning was conducted concerning the JIS-mark
labelling system. The results of the questioning were made public in April
1983.

b) Comparative Testing

33.   The Japan Consumer Information Center conducted comparative tests on 24
items including automobiles and electric razors between February 1983 and
January 1984, and made public the test results through its magazine
"Tashikana-me" (Critical Eyes) and other publications.

34.   The Japan Consumer's Association, with subsidies from the Ministry of
International Trade and Industry, conducted comparative tests on the quality
and performance of 24 items including videocassette recorders and binoculars,
and simple tests on four new products between February 1983 and January 1984.
The results of these were made public through the Association's magazine
"Gekkan Shohisha" (Monthly review for Consumers) and other media.

35.   The Japan Consumer Information Center prepared a comparative information report on consumer life entitled "Comparison of Home Delivery Services"
which was published in April 1983. The object of this report was to gather
information concerning the contents of individual home delivery services, complaints about the services, and the settlement of accidents and to provide
consumers with information given by home delivery service companies.

c) Advisory Services

36.   Most consumer complaints about products and services are settled
through bilateral negotiations between consumers and business enterprises,
such as retail stores. In addition, public organs, the Japan Consumer Information Center and Local Consumer Centers also handle such complaints and
grievances. The number of grievance and consultation cases received by these
public settlement organs totalled about 233 000 between April 1982 and March
1983. If this figure is added to the number of complaints and grievances received by consumer groups, the total number of cases reached about 236 700, up
13.9 per cent over the previous fiscal year. Classifying these complaints by
content, an increase in the number concerning sales methods, contracts and
services was particularly noticeable.

37.   The Ministry of Agriculture, Forestry and Fisheries and the Ministry of
International Trade and Industry have sections offering advisory services regarding consumer complaints. Between April 1982 and March 1983, the former
received 1 874 complaints and the latter 6 484 cases.

38.   The Ministry of International Trade and Industry is promoting the "system of qualification and registration of advisers on consumer life". The purpose of this system is to secure personnel who will be engaged in consumer consultation work mainly within enterprises, and who can motivate enterprises to reflect consumers' concerns in their business activities. In April 1983, the third group of 187 advisers on consumer life qualified, bringing the total number of qualified advisers to 579.

39.   In addition, the "system of qualifying textile quality control technicians", has been promoted by the Ministry of International Trade and Industry to secure personnel in enterprises engaged in the manufacture or sale of textile goods, whose job is to avoid occurrences of product quality deficiencies which lead to consumer complaints. In November 1983, the second group of 159 textile quality control technicians was qualified, bringing the total number of technicians to 539.

d) Mass Media

40.   In order to enable consumers to make rational consumer decisions, to genuinely adapt the consumer policy administration to the needs of consumers and to promote the organisation of consumers, various ministries and government agencies in 1983 provided consumers with information on consumer protection measures, commodities, services and contracts through various media such as TV, radio and pamphlets, following the measures taken in the past.

e) Other Information Activities

41.   The Japan Consumer Information Center and Local Consumer Centres provide various kinds of information concerning the improvement of consumer life through periodicals and exhibitions, as well as through various kinds of mass media.

3. Consumer Education

42.   School education concerning consumer life is carried out in subjects such as household and social studies in accordance with the Ministerial Syllabus for elementary, lower secondary and upper secondary schools.

43.   Consumer leaders, who play a prominent part in educational activities concerning consumer problems, are gaining in importance due to the increased organisation of consumers. Furthermore, the prefectural authorities, cabinet-order specified cities and the Japan Consumer Information Center have been making efforts to nurture such leaders by providing training courses and lectures. In addition, some local Consumer Centres have been providing opportunities for consumer education by conducting correspondence educational courses.

4. Redress and Complaints Facilities

44.   The Ministry of Health and Welfare and the Adverse Drug Reaction Sufferings Relief Fund have tried to publicise the relief system for adverse drug

reaction sufferings and to promote the redress of adverse drug reaction sufferings through the smooth implementation of the system. In 1983, the number
of relief benefit payments requests made to the Adverse Drug Reaction Sufferings Relief Fund was 85 and the number of payments was 45.

45.   Studies were made on the increase of the items to be covered by the
home electric appliance liability insurance as well as on the improvement and
expansion of the system. As of August 1983, the number of items covered by
the insurance was 25.

III. RELATIONS BETWEEN CONSUMER POLICY AND OTHER ASPECTS OF GOVERNMENTAL POLICY

1. Governmental Policy for Price Stabilization

46.   Price stability is a basic factor for the stabilization of people's
lives and a basis for the management of the national economy. From this
standpoint, the government attempted to maintain the stabilization of prices
by carrying out the following measures in 1983, designed to:

   i) Appropriately manage the general demand level;

   ii) Promote competition policy;

   iii) Fully utilise import policy;

   iv) Promote rationalization of low-productivity sectors and distribution business;

   v) Stabilize the supply of daily necessities and maintain their proper prices;

   vi) Keep public utility charges under strict control;

   vii) Study and keep watch on the supply-demand and price movements of
products and materials directly related to consumer life.

Due to the drop in crude oil prices and other favourable conditions, the consumer price index for 1983 rose 1.9 per cent, the lowest rise since 1959 when
a 1.0 per cent increase was registered.

2. Competition Policy

47.   The Fair Trade Commision takes measures of "cease-and-desist order",
"warnings" and others in cases of excessive premiums and misleading representations violating the Act against Unjustifiable Premiums and Misleading Representations (hereinafter called the "Premiums and Representation Act"). In
1983, "cease-and-desist orders" were issued regarding three cases of premiums
and 9 cases of representations (12 cases in all). Important examples include
the case in which premiums exceeding the legal maximum value were presented to
participants in agent-organised tours and unjustifiable representations of

characteristics on real estate. Warnings were issued and other administrative measures of guidance were taken in 803 cases of premiums and 479 cases of representations (1 282 cases in all). In May 1983, the Commission, in co-operation with the national and municipal offices concerned, conducted a nationwide investigation on the presentation in real estate advertisements for the second consecutive year and regulated misleading representations violating the Premiums and Representations Act.

48.   Fair competition rules, voluntary regulatory rules concerning premiums and representations, have been firmly established in many industries and have been actively carried out. In 1983, rules concerning premiums for 11 items including magazines were approved by the FTC. As of January 1984, a total of 45 such rules existed. Furthermore, fair competition rules concerning representations were approved for two items including meat. As a result, as of January 1984, there was a total of 68 such rules.

49.   The Act Concerning Prohibition of Private Monopoly and Maintenance of Fair Trade has been strictly enforced in order to maintain fair and free competition. In 1983, the Fair Trade Commission issued decisions ordering the elimination of violating practices in 14 cases. Among the decisions, three cases were concerned with resale price maintenance of consumer goods, namely soft drinks and toys.

3. Conservation of Natural and Energy Resources

50.   The "Central Conference of National Movement of Conservation of Natural and Energy Resources" and the "Local Conference of National Movement of Conservation of Natural and Energy Resources" have been established to accelerate, in a national campaign, the saving of resources and energy. Since last year, spontaneous activities for the public enlightenment of resource and energy saving have taken place through meetings, lectures, distribution of pamphlets and posters, and so on.

51.   The government, in addition, has set February as "Energy Conservation Month" and the first day of each month as "Energy Conservation Day" and has carried out various energy conservation campaigns by distributing pamphlets and posters and through other activities to enlighten the public on resources and energy saving.

4. International Trade

52.   Since 1981, the government has established and implemented a series of external economic measures in order to maintain the free trade system and thus to promote global economic development. The nucleus of these measures is the domestic market opening measures, and as part of the market opening efforts, a comprehensive improvement measure concerning the Standard and Certification Systems was decided upon in March 1983. In addition, the "Law to Amend part of the Laws to Facilitate the Obtaining of Type Approval, etc. by Foreign Manufacturers" was promulgated in May 1983 and put into force in August of the same year in order to ensure non-discriminatory certification among domestic and foreign manufacturers. The law was formulated taking into account the importance of maintaining safety and other benefits for users of various products in the country.

53.   The government in October 1983 established Comprehensive Economic Measures at the Ministerial Conference for Economic Measures. It includes the following four items concerning opening up of markets:

    i) Reduction of tariff rates;

    ii) Further relaxation of import-restricting measures;

    iii) Firm implementation of improvement measures concerning Standard and Certification Systems;

    iv) Vigorous promotion of O.T.O. (Office of Trade Ombudsman) activities.

Import promotion measures have also been decided upon, including easier import finance and improved distribution system for imported goods. Other measures which have been decided upon included promotion of capital inflow and international transactions by the yen, and improvement in the conditions for financial and capital markets.

Budget for Consumer Administration

(in thousand yen)

Items	FY 1984 (A)	FY 1983 (B)	(A)-(B)	(A)/(B)
1. Accident prevention	3 445 131	4 174 806	-729 675	0.83
2. Correct weights and measures	3 555	3 741	-186	0.95
3. Standardization	927 024	1 000 753	-82 729	0.92
4. Proper labelling	211 598	204 230	7 368	1.04
5. Ensuring fair and free competition	194 321	195 132	-811	1.00
6. Proper contracts	120 730	122 362	-1 632	0.99
7. Consumer education	2 359 366	2 022 745	336 621	1.17
8. Reflection of consumers' opinions in administration	87 563	90 059	-2 496	0.97
9. Improvement of product testing and inspection facilities etc.	163 464	166 486	-3 022	0.98
10. Improvement of complaint handling systems	48 994	55 119	-6 125	0.89
11. Promotion of consumer organisations	189 550	225 100	-35 550	0.84
12. Others	3 228 307	3 418 661	-190 354	0.94
Total	10 979 603	11 688 194	-708 591	0.94

LUXEMBOURG

REGULATIONS AND OTHER PROVISIONS CONCERNING
CONSUMER PROTECTION, INFORMATION AND EDUCATION
AND APPEALS PROCEDURES

1. Consumer protection

a) Physical protection

1.   The Ministry of Health has, as is done each year, ordered the withdrawal of certain medicines harmful to consumers.

In January 1984, sales of Asiatic shrimps were prohibited: more flexibility is due to be introduced into the relevant order shortly.

b) Protection of the economic interests of consumers

2.   The Law of 25th August 1983 concerning legal protection of consumers is
designed to restore the balance between consumers and traders.   The text of
the Law sets out as examples a series of clauses to be considered as in breach
of the legislation and therefore null and void.   The Chairman of the Court of
the district in which the applicant is domiciled may, at the request of any
individual, professional group or consumers' association represented on the
Prices Commission, rule that a clause or a combination of clauses is in breach
of the Law, the case being brought before the court and an injunction issued.
The Law provides for the posting and publication of the decision and for a
substantial fine.   The Law also deals with the question of denunciation by
consumers of sales contracts negotiated by door-to-door salesmen, within seven
days of the order or undertaking to purchase and 14 days of reception of the
goods.

3.   Concerning the legislative activities of the Office of Prices, special
mention should be made of the following:

-- The Ministerial Order of 11.4.1983 fixing maximum prices for dairy
   products;

-- The Grand-Ducal Regulation of 11.4.1983 fixing normal prices for
   taxi journeys;

94

-- The Grand-Ducal Regulation of 10.5.1983 fixing maximum retail prices for fresh milk, fresh cream and butter;

-- The Ministerial Order of 27.5.1983 fixing maximum prices for dairy products;

-- The Ministerial Order of 24.6.1983 fixing maximum prices for dairy products;

-- The Grand-Ducal Regulation of 29.6.1983 fixing maximum retail selling prices for solid mineral fuels for domestic use;

-- The revisions of retail prices in cases where rates of VAT have been raised, dated 24.6.1983;

-- The Law of 7.7.1983 amending the Law of 30th June 1961 for the purpose inter alia of cancelling and replacing the Grand-Ducal Order of 8th November 1944 establishing an Office of Prices;

-- The Grand-Ducal Regulation of 17.8.1983 fixing the retail sale prices of pharmaceutical products of Belgian origin or provenance, and the profit margins of wholesalers and pharmacists;

-- The Grand-Ducal Regulation of 15.10.1983 concerning the adjustment of profit margins in absolute terms during the year 1983;

-- The Ministerial Order of 7.12.1983 fixing maximum retail prices for pre-packed potatoes;

-- The Ministerial Order of 10.1.1984 fixing maximum retail prices for pre-packed potatoes;

-- The Ministerial Order of 9.2.1984 fixing maximum retail prices for pre-packed potatoes;

-- The Ministerial Order of 9.3.1984 fixing maximum retail prices for pre-packed potatoes.

NETHERLANDS

I. INSTITUTIONAL DEVELOPMENTS IN THE FIELD OF CONSUMER POLICY

1.   At the time it came to office, the present Dutch Cabinet declared that consumer affairs, especially in the light of the current social and economic circumstances, deserved intensive care and attention from the Government. In accordance with this, and in a departure from the economies and personnel reductions which the Cabinet applied elsewhere, Holland's consumer affairs budget for 1984 was augmented by Gld 2 million (specifically for the advancement of consumer information via radio and television) and the workforce of the Directorate for Consumer Policy was increased as well.

2.   At present, in the Netherlands a broad discussion is taking place on the role and functioning of legislation. Two committees delivered advisory reports to the Government on this subject in the course of 1983. One of these was an interim report on the general conditions needed for simplifying and decreasing the amount of already-existing legislation and projected legal measures were examined with regard to the possibility of lightening the burden of taxes and contribution of Dutch industry. This report dealt in part with a number of regulations important to the consumer, such as projected legislation dealing with consumer protection, general conditions of sales and a bill calling for alterations in the Consumer Goods Act. On the basis of this report, the Government has decided to adapt a number of legal regulations and to withdraw the Sales Act. This latter withdrawal has already taken place. In line with this, the Government is at the moment (early 1984) considering two new reports dealing with deregulation. Consumer matters are dealt with in these reports as well. Consumer organisations are concerned about the possible effects of these deregulatory operations on the consumer's interests.

The Institute on Household Financial Planning

3.   The Institute on Household Financial Planning, which aims to provide consumers with information on budget problems related to income and spending, will be reorganised to permit a better management structure. A new director has been nominated and the government subsidy to the Institute has been increased. The Institute is developing consumer information on rational spending for the lower income categories.

The Foundation for Consumer Affairs Research (SWOKA)

4.   The Foundation for Consumer Affairs Research (SWOKA) has now been in operation for four years. SWOKA is led by the two general consumer organisations and is subsidised by four Ministries. The Foundation's research is intended to supply expertise and insight to be incorporated in the policies carried out by both the Government and the consumer organisations. For this reason, it is essential for the Foundation to be "tuned in" to the information needs of these organisations' policymakers. A recent evaluatory report showed that SWOKA more than met the requirements of scientific quality and policy relevance, but that programme procedures (especially the contact between SWOKA workers and policymakers) could be improved. Therefore, a new procedure has been agreed upon. SWOKA's workforce now totals 25 full-time and project assistants. Its subsidies at the moment amount to Gld 4 million.

In 1983, SWOKA published reports on:

-- Predictions of the possible effects of policy measures on consumption (English version);

-- Households and external facilities;

-- Household production and household activities;

-- Electrical consumption of five household appliances;

-- Consumption distribution (in contrast to Income Distribution);

-- Income developments and household activities;

-- Household electrical quotas;

-- Medical consumption.

Consumer Safety Foundation

5.   The Safety Section, formerly within the private sphere of the Safety Institute, went independent in 1983 as the Consumer Safety Foundation. In 1983, the Foundation received a government subsidy of some Gld 2.2 million. Among its most important activities are: the organisation of the national accident-registration system in 17 hospitals, research and supplying public and individual information. The latter is carried out partly by means of a telephone "advice-and-complaint line".

II. REGULATORY OR OTHER ACTION CONCERNING CONSUMER PROTECTION, INFORMATION AND EDUCATION, AND MEANS OF REDRESS

1. Consumer protection

a) Physical protection (product safety)

6.   Two new legal measures were taken in 1983 in the field of product safety, one dealing with the use of asbestos fibres in consumer goods, and one dealing with cosmetic products. Research was done on, among other things, poisoning accidents. This research was carried out by the Consumer Safety Foundation.

b) Protection of the consumer's economic interests

Consumer credit: effective interest rate

7.   As from 1st January 1984, indication of the effective rate of interest in advertisements and contracts on consumer credit is required.

Expert Group on Life Insurance

8.   The Expert Group on Life Insurance, consisting of representatives of life insurance companies, insurance brokers, consumer organisations and government officials, carried out studies on consumer problems with life insurance. An advisory report on establishing prospectuses for consumers was accepted unanimously. No agreement was reached on standardizing questionnaires and price-earning ratios in life insurance business. In the course of 1984, the Dutch Government will make decisions on the basis of these studies.

Evaluation of "Misleading Advertising" Law

9.   In accordance with a commitment made with the Dutch Parliament, an evaluatory report has been drafted -- after three years of experience with the Misleading Advertising Law -- on the experiences of consumer organisations with this law and the means for legal redress (Ius Agendi) supplied within the law. The report concluded that the misleading Advertising Law has functioned well. The law's action clause for consumer organisations appears to have functioned especially well in preventing law suits. The law also provides support for judgement by the Advertisement Code Commission (a self-regulatory body).

2. Consumer information

Product information on non-food

10.   The Consumer Affairs Commission of the Social and Economic Council, an important advisory body of the Dutch Government, issued an advisory report on the subject of product information in June of 1983. On the basis of this report, the Government drafted a memorandum on product information for non-foods which was presented to Parliament at the end of 1983. This memorandum emphasizes the Government's plans for improving product information. The Government will set up working groups, comprised of representatives of Dutch industry, consumer organisations and research institutes, charged with designing product information systems for specific products (product groups). The choice was made for a step-by-step approach. In 1984 activities will be started in the areas of household furnishings and textiles.

Household and consumer information

11.   At the time it came to office, the current Cabinet set itself the task of intensifying consumer information policy. In realising this task, both mass media information -- in particular, via radio and TV -- and "front line" information direct to the consumer were brought into play. With regard to the former, a consumer information radio and television project is in the making. This facility is expected to fill a supply function for broadcasting and other media, especially with regard to specific information expertise and to stimulating a more systematic follow-up within the range of the mass media. During the project's initial phase, two experimental information projects to be supplied by the consumer organisations have been subsidised for television. These projects have as their goal increasing consumers' "self-defence" by providing them with practical and manageable information.

12.   With regard to the "front line" information service, several small-scale information projects are being prepared in such a way that they will use the existing channels for education, information and advice for specific groups.

13.   Both information projects are intended not only to gain expertise and experience in the field of information methods directed to specific target groups, but also to monitor the desired co-operation between the various information strata.

Nutritional Information Office (VoVo)

14.   In co-operation with the Teleac televised educational service, VoVo has developed the eight part series "Proper Nutrition", broadcast in the spring of 1983. VoVo has recently increased its emphasis on developing educational material on nutritional matters for use in primary education.

3. Consumer education

15.   The Consumer's Association has begun, with a subsidy from the Dutch Ministry of Economic Affairs, to develop educational material in the field of adult education.

4. Redress and Complaints facilities

Branch arbitration committees

16.   The 1982 annual report of the Consumer Complaints Foundation showed 3 937 complaints registered with the eight arbitration committees associated with this Foundation. These were complaints on which the consumer and the business or service involved could not reach mutual agreement. 2 267 verdicts were handed down; of these, less than half (1 161) of the complaints were found to be partially or completely justified: the remainder were pronounced unfounded. Almost Gld 800 000 in damages on claims were awarded by the Arbitration Committee for Travel. 31 complaints were registered with the Fur Goods Guarantee Foundation's arbitration committee.

Simplified small claims court procedures

17.   At the end of September 1983, the Dutch Justice Ministry announced its decision to draft a bill aimed at simplifying court procedures for minor civil cases. The bill calls for cases involving less than Gld 5 000 to be committed for trial by filing a petition in accordance with a pre-established model. The written phase of the procedure remains, in principle, limited to this petition and a written defence. The cantonal judge is to be granted the authority to issue orders at any stage in the procedure, allowing him more control over the course of the procedure.

III. RELATIONS BETWEEN CONSUMER POLICY AND OTHER ASPECTS OF GOVERNMENTAL POLICY

18.   A research report has been completed on the methodology of Consumer Impact Statements and their possible function in the Dutch governmental context. Such statements are regarded as a new, potentially valuable policy tool and an instrument for the more systematic incorporation of consumer matters in proposed measures by all governmental departments. Discussions are still going on in order to reach a consensus on ways of implementing these statements. They will be carried out by the department responsible for the policy measure involved.

Environment

19.   The Government is currently making efforts to end the use of phosphates in detergents, taking into consideration the technical and economic possibilities including possible financial consequences for the consumer. On the basis

of agreements between government and industry, phosphate levels have been halved to 5 per cent as from 1983. After the results of this step have been analysed, further talks will be held with the goal of eliminating the use of phosphates by 1987.

Pricing policy

20.   Following the abolition of formal price-fixing regulations for most of trade and industry and a limited part of the service sector in 1983, even further relaxations of pricing regulations have been effected in 1984. Price-fixing regulations have been maintained or, as the case may be, effected for only a very limited number of sectors; price-fixing for the rest of trade and industry in 1984 can be regarded as unregulated. Nonetheless, government supervision of pricing developments will continue. Should these developments in certain sectors become undesirable and consultation with the sector involved fail to result in corrective measures, new price-fixing regulations could be effected.

Competition policy

21.   Parliamentary handling of the bill calling for changes in the Economic Competition Law is almost complete; among other things, the bill includes a regulation dealing with the open cartel register which calls for competitive arrangments to be made public.

NEW ZEALAND

I. INSTITUTIONAL DEVELOPMENTS

Small Claims Tribunals

1.   These tribunals provide a forum for the settlement of many consumer-trader disputes, without the formality or expense of court proceedings. Use may be made of them generally where the amount claimed is founded in contract, is disputed by the defendant and where the claim does not exceed $500. Tribunals were opened in five centres during 1983, bringing the total number of tribunals to 18.

II. NEW REGULATIONS OR MODIFICATIONS TO EXISTING LAWS

1. Consumer Protection

2.   An Insurance Law Reform Bill was introduced at the end of the 1983 parliamentary session for recess study. The bill provides additional protection for purchasers of houses prior to the transfer of possession, limits the use of average clauses in certain kinds of policies, clarifies the law on insuring minors, and makes provision for the payment of interest when there are delays in settling claims under life insurance policies.

3.   The Law Practitioners Act, which came into force on 1 April 1983, makes significant changes in the procedures for investigating complaints against solicitors. In particular, there is provision for review of complaints by a lay observer if the complainant is disatisfied with the outcome of an investigation.

4.   The Commerce Act was amended to modify procedures at expedite hearings by the Commerce Commission under that legislation.

5.   A new Toxic Substances Act and Toxic Substances Regulations came into force on 1 August 1983. They provide improved measures for the control of toxic substances by regulating their labelling, advertising, sale, distribution, transport, storage and import.

2. Consumer Information

6.   The Consumers' Institute handled 21,745 consumer complaints. It published the result of 30 comparative tests.

7.   The Accident Compensation Commission produced a technical report on product risk analysis techniques, providing ways of establishing product risk scores. The report is available for companies developing new products and those involved in product safety.

3. Consumer Education

8.   The news media took an increasing interest in consumer affairs. A weekly television programme, Fair Go, continued to attract widespread interest with its handling of complaints from members of the public.

9.   In co-operation with the Department of Education and the staff of secondary schools, the Consumers' Institute began a pilot programme aimed at incorporating consumer education in schools' curricula on a better developed basis than previously. In 1981, the Institute's quarterly publication for teachers to promote awareness of consumer issues in schools changed its name from "Teaching Notes" to "Consumer Action". In 1982, a survey was done on how much consumer education was being taught in schools. The findings of the survey will enable the development of suitable programmes of consumer education. In 1984, the Consumers' Institute appointed an Education Officer. This officer will spend three years working in the Department of Education preparing resources based on the findings of the 1982 survey. These resources will be prepared to fit into existing Social Studies, Economic Studies and Home Economics syllabuses.

III. CHANGES IN THE BUDGET ALLOCATED TO CONSUMER QUESTIONS

10.   The Government granted (through Vote Trade and Industry) $931,675 to the Consumers Institute, an increase of $34,125 over the previous year's grant.

IV. RELATIONS BETWEEN CONSUMER POLICY AND OTHER ASPECTS OF GOVERNMENT POLICY

1. Price Freeze

11.   A major contribution to price stability was made by the price freeze which continued in force throughout 1983 and was terminated on 29 February 1984. The freeze covered the great majority of sales of goods and services with the exception of goods traded at auction. Principal allowable grounds for exemption were rises in the price of imported content and economic hardship.

12.   In June 1982, the month the freeze was introduced, the annual rate of inflation as measured by the Consumers' Price Index stood at 17 percent. By 1 March 1984, that figure had fallen to 3.5 percent.

13.   During the freeze 8113 complaints were received about price rises by the Department of Trade and Industry. Of these 85 percent were found to be permissible increases in terms of the regulations. Of 2839 applications for exemptions under the freeze 61 percent were successful.

2. Price Surveillance System

14.   The freeze has been succeeded by a price surveillance system which remains in force for one year beginning 1 March 1984. During that period all manufacturers of goods and suppliers of services are limited to two price increases. In addition, major traders (i.e. manufacturers of goods with an annual turnover of $10 million and suppliers of services with an annual turnover of $3 million) are required to notify the Department of Trade and Industry before increasing the prices.

15.   The department has the authority to monitor and investigate any price increase and, if necessary, intervene by fixing reasonable prices for particular traders.

3. Energy conservation

16.   A number of firms involved in converting vehicles to run on CNG have agreed to apply performance guidelines established by the Ministry of Energy in conjunction with the motor trade when carrying out these conversions. These premises are identified by a special sticker.

17.   The main purpose of the programme is to ensure that the conversion of vehicles to CHG is carried out to a high standard of performance (safety requirements are laid down in legislation). This in turn will increase public confidence and should lead to an increase in the rate of conversion to this much lower cost, indigenous fuel.

18.   The Ministry of Energy is currently developing a publicity programme to give garages which have adopted the guidelines maximum exposure.

19.   During 1983, the Ministry of Energy published an illustrated book "How to Heat Your Home". It contains advice on simple steps which can be taken to get the best performance out of existing heating equipment and on choosing alternative forms of heating e.g. solar.

I. INSTITUTIONAL DEVELOPMENTS IN THE FIELD OF CONSUMER POLICY

1.   The Government put before the Parliament (Storting) a position paper on the future tasks and organisation of the consumer sector in March 1983.

The main points were:

-- Further decentralisation of the Consumer Council by more resources given to the local offices;

-- Dissolution of the Committee for Informative Labelling and the tasks given to the Consumer Council and the Consumer Ombudsman;

-- Reorganistion of the National Institute for Consumer Research was proposed.

2.   The Parliament approved in May 1983 as follows:

-- Further decentralisation of the Consumer Council is encouraged;

-- The Committee for Informative Labelling was disbanded from January 1984, and the tasks of the Committee have been taken over by the Consumer Council and the Consumer Ombudsman. As part of the work connected with compulsory and voluntary labelling and product information, a Contact Committee between the Consumer Council and the industry and trade organisations has been established. This body also has representatives from other consumer institutions. The Consumer Council acts as the secretariat for the Committee;

-- A reorganisation of the National Institute for Consumer Research was discussed. It was decided that a reorientation of the research should be carried out according to changing needs for knowledge of consumer-related problems.

II. REGULATORY OR OTHER ACTION CONCERNING CONSUMER PROTECTION, INFORMATION AND EDUCATION, AND MEANS OF REDRESS

1. Consumer Protection

a) Physical protection (Product safety)

Chemical Products

3.   Regulations concerning Labelling, Sale, etc. of Chemical Substances and Products which may involve a Hazard to Health entered into force on 1st March 1983. Producers and importers have had a one-year period of transition, until 1st March 1984, for classifying the products. The regulations are, in most respects, quite similar to the EEC regulations. General rules apply to main categories of substance and products such as very toxic, toxic, harmful, carcinogenic, corrosive, irritant and allergic. Under the system, any product, whether it consists of one or more substances, is subject to regulation. Products shall be classified as carcinogenic and labelled with a specific warning text when they contain 0.1 or more per cent of a carcinogenic substance. Such substances, which number 103, are listed separately.

Nuisances due to excess noise

4.   Regulations concerning maximum sound-power levels for bulldozers, excavators, loaders and lawn mowers were laid down by the Ministry of Environment in 1982. By January 1984, noise data on approximately 1 900 products were stored in the Data Bank. Priority has been given to information on construction equipment. A group under the aegis of the Nordic Council of Ministers is co-ordinating efforts to collect more data in this area.

Mechanical products -- Physical Protection

5.   Regulations concerning the flammability of textiles were laid down by the Ministry of Environment on 13th February 1984. The regulations prohibit the manufacture, importation, or sale of highly flammable apparel and certain textile products. The requirements are based on ASTM D 1230-61 (Standard Test Method for Flammability of Clothing Textiles), but the time of the flame spread is strengthened to 7.0 seconds for children's clothing and to 5.0 seconds for other clothing textiles. The regulations will enter into force on 1st September 1984, for children's clothing, and one year later for other textiles used in clothing.

6.   Norwegian standards concerning the mechanical, chemical and flammability aspects of toys have been issued. Guidelines for toys are under preparation as complements to the standards. These will also include the noise aspect.

7.   A specific type of double-handled bathroom equipment has been withdrawn from the Norwegian market. The equipment, of Norwegian origin, has caused several scalding accidents among small children.

8.   Specific action has been taken against several hazardous toys during 1983 such as "Water Snake", "Magic Egg" and erasers resembling food. These toys have been recalled from the Norwegian market through voluntary agreements with the toy industry.

9.   Safety has also been an important aspect of the Consumer Council's work concerning the sale of used cars. As a result, dealers of used cars, to an increasing extent, use objective condition reports. One producer, Fiat, agreed to apply to the Nordic antirust codex; six years' guarantee against rust and three years' guarantee for the car enamel. Five to six other importers have also agreed to introduce better guarantees in 1984.

10.   The new regulations (as from 1st January 1984) demanding safety belts for children in rear seats of cars add greatly to their safety in the case of accidents.

11.   The Nordic Council of Ministers finances research projects in the product safety field. During 1983 projects have been completed on: criteria for risk evaluation, bicycle accidents, flammability labelling of textiles, data collection of accidents (including an English summary), and an analysis of falls on the level (also including an English summary).

12.   A research project concerning recall actions has been carried out by the State Pollution Control Authority. This is the first part of the Norwegian contribution to a research project under the Nordic Council of Ministers.

13.   Another project, carried out by the State Pollution Control Authority, is studying the effectiveness of the recall action taken by the Norwegian producer of the bathroom equipment mentioned above. The study started in September 1983 and will be completed in early 1984.

14.   The National Institute for Consumer Research is doing research in several fields. Only a few are related to consumer protection and include a project on the influence of use and laundering on retro-reflective fabrics as well as a project on the influence of use and laundering on the flammability of flame retardant cotton.

b) Protection of consumers' economic interests

15.   The statute regulating door-to-door sales has been amended, and the scope of the act extended in such a way that it also encompasses telephone and mail order selling (Act of 3rd June 1983). According to the new statute, a consumer may renounce an order that he has placed either by mail order, telephone or through a sales representative outside his ordinary place of business, if he gives notice to the seller within ten days after he has received the commodity ordered.

16.   The right to renounce does not apply if the total cost of the goods ordered does not exceed NKr 200, nor does it apply to the sale of food or for orders placed by members of book clubs etc.

17.   The ten-day period does not start running until the commodity ordered is delivered and the buyer has received a special document by means of which he is reminded of his rights pursuant to the Act.

18.   By a modification in the Act regulating commerce of the same date, the right to solicit by door-to-door selling has been altered. It is not any longer necessary to seek permission. The local authorities may, however, prohibit such sales practices if the interest of the established commerce makes such a regulation necessary.

2. Consumer information

a) Comparative testing

19.   Comparative tests are used by the State Pollution Control Authority to evaluate a product from the safety point of view. This is necessary when drafting regulations and guidelines, or when the Authority wants to check whether products on the market comply with existing requirements. In 1983 such tests have been carried out for skiing equipment, toys and safety helmets.

20.   The Consumer Council reports that 14 comparative tests of goods and services were made during 1983. The results were published in Forbruker-rapporten (Consumer Report), a periodical issued ten times a year. Among the tests carried out are tests on household appliances, bicycles and the safety of pleasure boats.

21.   The general technical quality of many consumer goods has reached an acceptable level and more attention has, therefore, been focused on durability, repair frequencies and servicing organisation. A representative group of readers of the Consumer Report were asked about their experience with washing machines during autumn 1983. The results from this and other consumer surveys planned for the near future will form a basis for influencing the production and servicing of consumer goods.

b) Advisory services

22.   Most of the advisory service of the Consumer Council is given by its 18 regional consumer offices. In 1983, they received 26 000 applications from consumers asking for pre-purchase and other advice. An additional 5 000 applications came to the central secretariat.

c) Mass media

23.   The Consumer Council makes use of direct contacts with the television and radio of the national broadcasting company, and this has resulted in several programmes on consumer problems. Press releases based on articles in the Consumer Report have been extensively published, especially in the regional and local newspapers. Press releases based on decisions and opinions of the governmental consumer bodies are also widely used by the mass media.

d) Other information activities

24.   Sales and distribution of informative material is an important part of the consumer institutions' information activities. Forbruker-rapporten (Consumer Report) has a special position as a consumer periodical for general

distribution. The number of subscribers reached a maximum six years ago (249 000 subscriptions), but has since then been reduced to 183 000 subscribers in 1983. An increase of the subscription rate can only be part of the explanation, since this rate is still very low. The Council is considering measures to increase the number of subscribers.

25.   Electronic payment systems are about to be introduced in the retail trade. The Consumer Council has arranged a conference to discuss problems and advantages of this new technology.

26.   The State Pollution Control Authority is planning an information programme which will enable the Authority to reach a greater number of consumers. The Authority also takes an active part in conferences and exhibitions. Information material such as brochures and booklets have been published to make consumers aware of their rights in connection with safety of products. The Authority also encourages consumers to submit information on products involved in accidents or of other experiences related to product safety.

27.   A project on the establishment of a product data bank was carried out in 1983 by the State Pollution Control Authority. This work will continue in 1984.

3. Consumer education

28.   Consumer education has for ten years been an obligatory subject in elementary schools in Norway. It has, however, no place of its own on the time-table, and is dependent on being taught in connection with other subjects or as a special project. Good teaching aids are important for efficient consumer education. The consumer institutions have produced some material, but this is still not sufficient to make the teaching of consumer education effective.

29.   On the Nordic level, a project on consumer education at teachers' training colleges was completed in the autumn of 1982. The project has resulted in recommendations to regional teachers' training colleges on how consumer education can be taught as an obligatory subject in elementary schools.

20.   The State Pollution Control Authority has in 1983 set up an exhibition which is used at seminars and conferences to inform different groups of consumers about safety products for home and leisure time.

31.   As a co-operation project within the Nordic Council, the National Institute for Consumer Research has carried out an analysis of commercial teaching material used in public schools.

4. Redress and complaints facilities

32.   The Consumer Council received 80 000 complaints in 1983. About 90 per cent of them came to the regional offices. Four thousand seven hundred of them were handled as registered complaint cases. In 50 per cent of these cases, consumers were given some kind of redress. The average time of handling is five months.

33.   Cases which are not solved by the Consumer Council's mediation and advice, are brought before the Consumers' Civil Disputes' Committee -- a small claims court for consumer complaints. Four hundred and sixteen cases were thus taken up by the CCDC in 1983. Decisions were made in 256 cases, five of them after processing in the ordinary courts.

34.   The Consumer Council arranged a conference on patients' legal rights in October 1983.

III. RELATIONS BETWEEN CONSUMER PLICY AND OTHER ASPECTS OF GOVERNMENTAL POLICY

35.   The Consumer Ombudsman has continued the work for better contract terms especially concerning the sale of prefabricated houses, conditions for loans from banks and other credit institutions, and contracts on cable television instalment and after-instalment service.

36.   Concerning marketing practices, the Ombudsman has concentrated on regulating the marketing of slimming products and sex discriminatory advertising, especially of products which in itself may be claimed discriminatory (video, magazines).

37.   The control of misleading price advertising, and unsubstantiated claims as to quality for several product groups, have also had priority.

38.   The State Pollution Control Authority, under the Ministry of Environment, has the main administrative responsibility for the implementation of the Product Control Act of 1976.

39.   Act No. 6 of 13th March 1981 concerning Protection against Pollution and concerning Waste (Pollution Control Act) will enter into force on 1st October 1984. This law includes the most important regulations concerning pollution and waste.

I. INSTITUTIONAL DEVELOPMENTS IN THE FIELD OF CONSUMER POLICY

1.   Following the approval of the Consumer Protection Act in 1981, 1983 was another important landmark for the protection of the consumer in Portugal. The functions of the Ministry for the Quality of Life (MQV) were defined by a Decree-law early in 1983. In the introduction to that measure it is stated that "the living standard of the population also involves consumer protection in the broadest sense and includes the protection of those at whom advertising is directed. It is therefore logical that the Ministry for the Quality of Life should be the government department responsible, in co-ordination with other government departments, for effectively developing an extended and coherent policy to safeguard the legitimate rights and interests of the consumer".

2.   The responsibilities of the MQV in regard to consumer protection are to:

-- Study, promote and participate in a policy to safeguard the rights and interests of the consumer, either for the purposes of consumer protection, or for the purposes of planning and implementing normative and preventive action;

-- Collaborate in the formulation and approval of Portuguese regulations reflecting the consumer protection standpoint.

3.   To carry out these responsibilities a Consumer Protection Bureau (BDC) was set up within the MQV as a technical support service. The MQV is also responsible for the National Consumer Protection Institute (INDC) which has its own legal personality and administrative autonomy.

4.   The INDC and the BDC were also the subject of regulations passed early in 1983, and the BDC began its activity in the same year. The INDC started its activity in 1984.

5.   INDC. The Institute is charged with studying, co-ordinating and giving effect to consumer protection, information and education measures and giving support to consumer organisations, having regard to the need to protect consumers against goods and services prejudicial to their health and safety, the special characteristics of the most underprivileged consumer groups and regional consumption patterns. To this end the INDC has the following functions:

111

-- To examine and make proposals to the government on the definition of consumer protection policies;

-- To examine and promote technical and financial support arrangements for consumer protection organisations;

-- To examine and promote special support programmes for the most underprivileged consumers, especially the elderly, the handicapped and those with meagre economic resources;

-- To stimulate and propose consumer training and education measures;

-- To establish regular contacts with similar bodies abroad and promote joint action to protect the consumer, especially in regard to training and education;

-- In general, to promote the application of measures introduced by Act No. 29/81 of 22nd August 1981.

6. The organs of the INDC are the General Council, the Director and the Board of Administration. The Institute is managed by the General Council which consists of seven members designated as follows:

-- 2 by Parliament;

-- 2 by the Government;

-- 2 by generally representative consumer associations;

-- 1 by consumer co-operatives.

The General Council is responsible for:

-- Establishing principles for the preparation of the annual programme of activities and the INDC budget, as well as programmes and budgets covering several years and any amendments made to them;

-- Submitting the above documents to the Ministry for the Quality of Life for approval, together with the annual report and management accounts, without prejudice to any decision by the Audit Office;

-- Following up INDC activities.

The INDC includes the following departments:

-- Training and Information Services Directorate;

-- Consumer Support Services Directorate;

-- Administrative Services Directorate;

-- Technical Studies Division;

-- Documentation Centre.

7.   <u>BDC</u>. This is a technical support service of the Minister working in conjunction with the INDC, to enable the government to pursue an overall consumer protection policy. It helps co-ordinate action between government departments to ensure the formulation and development of an extended and coherent policy and will provide appropriate legislative support. In addition, the BDC will be charged with protecting the interests of the consumer both as concerns the correct orientation of consumption and as concerns advertising, in close collaboration with the Advertising Council. The duties, organs and services of the BDC are defined in the implementing regulation attached (Annex).

8.   <u>ADVERTISING COUNCIL</u> (CP). A new formulation of the legal rules governing advertising (Decree-law No.303/83 of 28th June 1983) has given the CP a new constitution and structure. The Council and its executive board receive technical and administrative assistance from the BDC. The CP is an advisory and educational body in the field of advertising. It consists of representatives of government departments concerned with consumer protection, social communication, health, trade in foodstuffs and other goods, women's education and conditions, and representatives of consumers, and advertising and communication firms.

The CP is charged with:

-- Proposing principles to underlie consumer protection policy in regard to advertising;

-- Checking on application of the relevant legislation and reporting practices or action likely to contravene the law, either on its own initiative or following complaints made to it;

-- Giving its opinion on all legislative measures in regard to advertising;

-- Proposing a co-ordinated action programme, subject to assessment and review, to reduce the harmful effects of advertising;

-- Taking educational action through proposals for recommendations to improve the quality of advertising;

-- Protecting national advertising through directives aimed at gradually increasing the proportion in each of the media;

-- Preparing annually, before 31st March of the following year, a general report on the situation in the advertising field and on its own activity, for publication.

9.   <u>ANTI-SMOKING COUNCIL</u> (CPT). This Council was set up by Decree-law 226/83 of 27th May 1983 under the MQV. It is an inter-ministerial committee and consumers are represented on it through the INDC; the Council receives administrative support from the BDC.

The functions of the CPT are as follows:

-- To formulate, in line with the recommendations of international organisations, guiding principles for a policy to prevent smoking;

-- To propose a co-ordinated action programme subject to on-going assessment and review, designed progressively to reduce the harmful effects of smoking on the population; the programme will give priority to the protection of the rights of non-smokers and will give special attention to persons under age, through research, legislation and educational activities;

-- To act as an advisory body to the government in connection with the prevention of tobacco addiction;

-- To give its opinion on all legislation, action programmes and budgets concerned with the prevention of tobacco addiction;

-- To promote, follow and support studies, research and all action concerned with the prevention of tobacco addiction, with the aim in particular of identifying substances that tobacco should not contain or give off when consumed;

-- To ensure, in collaboration with the appropriate government departments, that the present decree is implemented, by reporting practices or action likely to violate it, either on its own initiative or as a result of complaints made to it;

-- To make arrangements for the exchange of knowledge, experience and techniques with similar bodies in other countries or with international organisations, with a view to stepping up international collaboration in the prevention of tobacco addiction;

-- To prepare annually, before 31st March of the following year, a general report on the current situation and on its own activity for publication.

10. NATIONAL QUALITY COUNCIL (CNQ). The CNQ has been set up under the Ministry for Industry, Energy and Exports and forms part of the national quality management system (Decree-law 165/83 of 27th April 1983). Consumers are once again represented on this council by the GDC, as a permanent delegate of the government, and by two members designated from among users and consumers: one by INDC and another by the respective associations; these two members have a three year renewable mandate.

The CNQ is responsible for:

-- Discussing standardization plans and programmes, particularly those to be included in policies and programmes to improve quality;

-- Adopting general methodology for the formulation and approval of rules of joint or private bodies concerned with standardization in each industry and for systems for the approval of bodies taking part;

-- Deciding problems of interpretation arising among bodies concerned with standardization and approval of standards;

-- Giving its opinion on policies and programmes to improve quality;

-- Proposing appropriate legislation and examining, as and when requested by the government, proposed legislation or regulations concerning methodology, standardization and approval.

11.   ADVISORY COMMITTEE ON COMPETITION (CCC). This Committee was set up by the law on competition (Decree-law 422/83 of 3rd December 1983) and will work alongside the Competition Council (set up by the same law under the Ministry for Trade and Tourism). It will consist of representatives of industry, agriculture and commerce, and representatives of consumers as determined by the Ministry. The CCC is responsible for giving its views on competition legislation and on other matters concerning practices in restraint of competition submitted to it by the Ministry for Trade and Tourism or by the Competition Council.

12.   BUDGET APPROPRIATIONS. As regards budget appropriations for matters concerning consumers the only figures available are those for the BDC, i.e. to Esc 27 586 000 for 1983. This mainly consisted of expenditure on setting up the service.

II. REGULATIONS AND OTHER MEASURES CONCERNING CONSUMER PROTECTION, INFORMATION AND EDUCATION, AND CONSUMER REMEDIES

1. Consumer protection

13.   Based on amendments introduced by the new Portuguese Penal Code, 16th May saw the publication of Decree-law No. 191/83 which may be seen, although indirectly, as forming part of a policy to protect the health and safety and the economic interests of consumers.

14.   As part of its health and safety provisions, this law provides for the withdrawal of foodstuffs likely to prejudice the health of or cause injury to consumers, by means of a system of administrative penalties involving the imposition of fines on transactors who fail to comply with rules concerning the purity, quality or composition of foodstuffs or food additives or animal feed. Economic interests are protected by the imposition of fines where goods are sent unrequested, where weighing and measuring equipment is defective or where there is incorrect display or price marking.

15.   However, this law has scarcely been applied due to the drafting of a proposed amendment to Decree-law No. 41/204, in force since 1957, dealing with offences against public health and the national economy. The proposed amendment led to the publication early in 1984 of Decree-law No. 28/84 (of 20th January) which repealed the 1957 legislation and the more recent Decree-law 191/83. Decree-law 28/84 will come into force on 1st March 1984.

16.   The new legislation also concerns consumer health and safety and the protection of their economic interests and imposes penalties for the following offences:

        -- Unlawful slaughtering;

        -- Contamination of goods;

-- Breaches of regulations concerning the purity, quality or composition of foodstuffs and food additives or of animal feed;

-- Monopoly or refusal to sell;

-- Speculation;

-- Misleading advertising.

17.   Fines are also provided for cases involving the sending of unrequested goods, absence of weighing and measuring equipment, defective display and price marking, non-approved prices and the misleading of consumers in connection with cut-price sales and similar practices.

18.   Since Decree-law 28/84 introduces an administrative procedure without intervention by the courts it makes for more rapid investigation and punishment of abuses.

19.   NATIONAL QUALITY MANAGEMENT SYSTEM.   Since this system also concerns the protection of the health and safety and economic interests of consumers it may be appropriate to refer to it here (the Decree-law involved was mentioned in paragraph 10). To promote a policy to maintain the quality of products and services, the Decree-law introduces and applies rules to protect public health and the safety of persons and goods, to protect the environment, to protect consumers and to improve working conditions.

20.   The system will be implemented nationwide on three levels: weights and measures, standardization, and approval. Each of these will involve stricter application of the rules, preparation of rules and other normative measures at national, regional, and international level, and action to ensure that products, services and undertakings comply with pre-established standards.

a) Consumer health and safety

21.   As regards foodstuffs mention should be made of the adoption of several Portuguese regulations concerning methods for the analysis of milk and plastic material used for handling and packaging foodstuffs, and on the definition, characteristics and packaging of edible oil, sausages, mortadella, cheese, fruit and frozen horticultural produce.

22.   The following decrees have also been published in the Official Gazette:

-- Decree-law No. 6/83 of 14th January 1983 fixing the maximum limit of permitted aflatoxins in foodstuffs;

-- Decree-law No. 221/83 of 26th May 1983 which regulates the marketing of animal feed;

-- Government Decree No. 83/83 of 9th December 1983 regulating the characteristics of yogurt and updating quality criteria.

23.   As regards consumer goods other than foodstuffs approvals continued in regard to domestic and industrial gas heating appliances and covered about 500 prototypes.   This means that all these appliances will bear the mark "PROTOTIPO" guaranteeing the safety of the consumer in the course of their use.

116

24.   Action was also taken to check quality and approve industrial goods.
notably tyres, ceramics (checks on cadmium and lead content), fertilizers,
electric and electronic equipment in games and toys.

25.   As regards games and toys, parts 1 and 2 of European Standard EN71 (approved by the European Standardization Committee to which Portugal belongs)
have been given consideration with a view to subsequent publication as
Portuguese standards.

26.   Legislation has been published (Decree-law No. 399/83 of 8th November
1983 and Order No. 929/83 of 22nd November 1983) to deal with possible irregu-
larities in domestic appliances for the supply of gas, including in tourist
and other accommodation.

27.   As part of the system of informal notification set up by Working Group
No. 3 of the OECD's Consumer Policy Committee, on the safety of consumer
goods, the BDC took action as a result of Notification No. 281 received by the
Organisation and concerning the "Lanzador" toy pistol manufactured by a
Spanish firm.   Steps taken by the BDC revealed that 150 pistols of this type
had entered Portugal. Since there is no special legislation providing for the
withdrawal of a dangerous article of this type, the BDC reached an agreement
with the importer providing for the withdrawal from the market of most of
these toy pistols and the suspension of imports. Meanwhile the public was
alerted through the media and attention drawn to the risks to children of
playing with these pistols.

b) Protection of the economic interests of consumers

i) Trading practices for goods and services (advertising and sales
   practices)

28.   Important legislation was published concerning advertising in 1983
(Decree-law No. 303/83 of 28th June). This Decree defines hidden, misleading,
comparative and door-to-door advertising, lays down principles with which advertising must comply, specifies advertising which is prohibited and cases in
which it must be limited or comply with predetermined conditions, and provides
for the punishment of offences.

29.   Other measures are found in the following legislation:

-- Order No. 962/83 of 5th November 1983 which forbids the sale of un-
   packed rice and specifies how packaging is to be marked;

-- Order No. 1028/83 of 9th December 1983 imposing compulsory price
   display, in precise and legible form, for services provided in all
   cafés, tea rooms etc.

This Decree also makes it obligatory to provide the consumer with a receipt
even though not requested.

30.   An Order of the Ministers for Trade and Tourism and for the Quality of
Life has set up a working group to examine and make proposals for the regulation of cut-price and winding-up sales. The group consists of representatives

of the BDC and of the general directorates for trade, competition and prices and the inspectorate for economic activities.

ii) Contractual relations between suppliers and consumers of goods and services

31.   In this area reference should be made to the applic   n of two codes of conduct introduced at the end of 1982 in the motor vehi   d electrical household appliance sectors.

32.   The Code of Conduct in the motor vehicle trade has been subscribed to by the ACP (Portuguese Automobile Club) and by the ACAP (Portuguese Motor Vehicle Trade Association) and covers both new and second-hand vehicles. According to information received from the associations, the Code has had positive results since in 1983 the number of complaints declined significantly. The results suggested that most complaints could be resolved by the supplier and the consumer without intervention by the associations. Only two cases were examined and were decided in favour of the consumer.

33.   The Code of Conduct for after sales service for electrical household appliances was subscribed to by the Portuguese Consumer Protection Association (DECO), by the Association of Wholesalers of Electrical, Photographic and Electronic Equipment (AGEFE) and by the National Association of Electric and Electronic Equipment Firms (ANIMEE). The associations involved are not aware of any complaints under the Code.

2. Consumer information

a) Labelling

i) Compulsory labelling

34.   A draft Decree-law was prepared on the labelling of foodstuffs to specify the conditions to be met by labelling of foodstuffs supplied to the end consumer, prepacked or otherwise, and to regulate presentation and advertising. This bill is expected to be approved shortly.

35.   Order No. 741/83 of 2nd July 1983 specifies warnings and information on amounts of harmful substances contained in tobacco to be printed on all cigarette packets.

b) Comparative testing

36.   The DECO and the consumer co-operative "Novos Pioneiros" (Braga) have done some work in this field. The work of the co-operative concerned the analysis of weight, composition, labelling, packaging and prices of products such as toothpaste, washing-up liquid, sugar, refrigerants, shampoos, butter and milk. The DECO has published studies on sales conditions and the use of products, notably solar collectors, hot water accumulators and bath heaters, surf boards and household insurance.

c) Advisory services

37.   The inspectorate for economic activities (in the Ministry of Trade and Tourism) continued its examination of complaints by consumers in regard to speculation, product quality, rents, etc. and has continued to provide information.

d) The media

38.   On the basis of the collaboration between the MQV and the Portuguese Radio, broadcasts have continued on consumer protection and proper nutrition.

39.   Under the auspices of the Food Education Commission (part of the Council for Food and Nutrition -- CAN) 14 television programmes and several other radio programmes have been made. Articles on the topic "Food and Health" have been released to the regional press.

e) Other information activities

40.   Other information has been put out by the magazine "PROTESTE" (published by the Consumers' Association), by the bulletins of some consumer co-operatives and by articles published in the press on the topic "Consumer Protection" and written by Mr. Beja Santos.

3. Consumer education

41.   The Commission for education and research on food, nutrition and health (another body of the CAN) has begun to investigate possible intervention in medical training courses and other higher education.

42.   As a result of contacts established with basic and primary schools, the "Novos Pioneiros" co-operative has given its support, in the field of food and consumer protection education, to activities by pupils and teachers.

43.   Theoretical and practical courses on food education have been given for the benefit of the adult population. These courses take place in the north of the country with the collaboration of the "Novos Pioneiros" co-operative, the Nutrition Association of Porto and the General Directorate for Adults of the Education Ministry.

44.   As part of action to prevent tobacco addiction education activities have been planned for implementation as from 1984.

4. Redress and complaints facilities

45.   In Decree-law No. 28/84 (referred to in paragraph 9 above) consumer associations are given the right to intervene as civil parties in criminal proceedings. Consumer associations may also take part in proceedings for other offences, when they so request, may submit memoranda and expert opinions and may request examinations or other steps to obtain evidence pending the final decision in the case.

46.   In regard to the complaints procedure the INDC has power to:

-- Assist individual consumers and especially the most underprivileged
   by giving information and accepting and dealing with suggestions and
   complaints;

-- Adapt procedures to the settlement of minor disputes in the consumer
   field.

47.   The Advertising and Anti-smoking Councils are also responsible for
looking into complaints made to them and reporting practices and action which
may be in breach of the regulations. In this connection the Councils may also
make recommendations or bring proceedings.

III. RELATIONS BETWEEN CONSUMER POLICY AND OTHER ASPECTS OF GOVERNMENT POLICY

1. Price stability

48.   In regard to price policy it should be noted that the unfavourable economic situation and the continued removal of price controls led to price
changes and successive price increases for consumers, particularly for certain
essential items, thus reducing the purchasing power of the Portuguese consumer.

2. Competition

49.   The Competition Act was published early in the year (Decree-law
No. 422/83 of 3rd December) and is to come into force in June 1984. But the
same Decree also set up the Competition Council and its Advisory Board. This
legislation is concerned, first, to eliminate the harmful economic effects of
cartels or the abuse of dominant positions and, second, to prohibit certain
individual practices in restraint of competition -- minimum prices, discriminatory prices or conditions and the buying back of goods or services.

3. Environmental protection

50.   In this field government action concerned the following:

-- The conclusion of negotiations with the EEC on the environment and
   consumer protection issue;

-- Publication of a Decree-law prohibiting the manufacture of dichloro-
   difluormethane and trichlorofluormethane and imposing import quotas;

-- Commencement of work leading to the creation of several commissions
   to control atmospheric pollution and protect the environment;

-- Commencement of work to draw up an outline Act on the environment
   and noise legislation.

4. Energy consumption

51.   The energy savings campaign continued through the media: television, radio, newspapers and magazines. This campaign drew the attention of the public in particular to domestic energy consumption with emphasis on lighting. It is believed that the campaign aroused interest among young people and consideration is being given to introducing the topic in schools in 1984.

5. International trade

52.   The BDC participated in the OECD's Consumer Committee in its work on consumer policy and international trade leading up to a seminar to be held in November 1984. To examine this question from the standpoint of the Portuguese consumer, the BDC has suggested the setting up of a working group consisting of representatives of the BDC and the Ministries of Finance and Planning, Trade and Tourism, the Sea and Agriculture, Forestry and Food.

6. Prevention of tobacco addiction

53.   With the aim of protecting the health of consumers and non-smokers affected by smoke in their environment, the Portuguese Government has by Decree-law No. 226/83, referred to in Chapter 1 of this report, prohibited smoking on public transport and in other public places, and has regulated cigarette advertising and required cigarette packets to carry warnings of dangers to health together with an indication of the nicotine and tar content of cigarettes. The same Decree also provides, in accordance with proposals by the Anti-Smoking Council, for a "co-ordinated action programme progressively to reduce the harmful effects of tobacco on the population (...) through investigation, legislation and education".

7. Food-nutrition-health

54.   Studies have been undertaken on consumption of foodstuffs containing sugar, especially cakes and refrigerants, in educational establishments and on the hawking of such products in schools. As a result of these studies a list of recommended foodstuffs has been prepared to be supplied in school canteens. A standard menu has been proposed for meals served in civil service and state enterprise canteens. An assessment has also been made, in the interests of the health of the population, of the need to make bread containing wheat and rye flour. It should be noted that all the above proposals still await a government decision.

SPAIN

I. INSTITUTIONAL DEVELOPMENTS IN CONSUMER POLICY

1.   The structural changes in 1983 in the administrative departments dealing with consumer affairs were as follows:

-- Creation of a Health and Consumer Action Unit (Unidad de Accion Sanitaria y de Consumo), in accordance with Royal Decree 41/1983 of 12th January, responsible for taking preventive action where a genuine risk exists and to co-ordinate resources and administration. The unit must also take all necessary steps to deal with crisis situations and emergencies facing the Ministry.

-- Creation of the Interministerial Commission to co-ordinate administrative inspection services for durable and consumer goods and services. (Royal Decree 1427/1983 of 25th May.) The Secretary-General for Consumer Affairs is Chairman of the Commission. His principal role is to co-ordinate the activities of the inspection services of various Ministries, of the Autonomous Communities and of provincial and municipal authorities so as to achieve maximum effectiveness.

2.   The practical functions of the Commission are as follows:

i) To establish and constantly update an inventory of the different central Government departments responsible for surveillance and control of foodstuffs and other goods and services for consumption or human use, as well as the human and material resources of those departments.

ii) To establish inspection or control plans to be prepared by means of co-ordination between the departments of central government involved, and, if necessary, promote joint activities with the Autonomous Communities and provincial and municipal authorities.

iii) To encourage and facilitate the definition of official methods of analysis for non-foodstuffs intended for human use or consumption and suggest studies and activities aimed at standardizing technical criteria and operating techniques of laboratories and installations.

iv) To draw up plans for training and further professional training in the field of inspection and quality control.

-- Updating of the composition of the Inter-ministerial Commission for Standardization and Approval, with a new formulation of its aims and functions intended to increase the effectiveness of its action.

-- As a result of the continuing transfer of central Government responsibility for consumer protection and market discipline to the Autonomous Communities, new administrative units have been created for the purpose of developing consumer policy in the different Autonomous Communities.

-- In addition, the Government has pursued a policy of collaboration and technical assistance between central Government and the provincial and municipal authorities. In 1983, 133 municipalities received economic aid from the Ministry of Health and Consumer Affairs in order to create local consumer information offices, install laboratories, introduce education programmes, etc. The total amount is shown in the Annex to the report.

-- In 1983 ten new consumer organisations were set up and entered in the register of the Instituto Nacional del Consumo -- one at regional level, five at provincial level and four at local level.

II. REGULATIONS AND OTHER ACTIVITIES CONCERNING CONSUMER PROTECTION, EDUCATION AND INFORMATION AND REMEDIES AVAILABLE

3.   Before reviewing practical activities, emphasis must be placed on progress achieved by the preparatory works on the future General Act on Consumer and User Protection. After studying the opinions it requested from institutions, ministries and bodies representing production and distribution, and consumers, the Government has adopted the Bill and submitted it to Parliament.

4.   This Bill seeks to recast, amend and adapt currently widely dispersed rules to the new structure of the State pursuant to Article 51 of the Spanish Constitution on express recognition of consumers' legitimate rights and protection of those rights by effective procedures. At the same time it creates a legal framework to facilitate optimal development of associations in this field.

1. Consumer protection

5.   Pursuant to the parliamentary mandate of 17th September 1981, the Government considered it appropriate to reshape and update the regulations in force concerning inspection and punishment of offences under Royal Decree 1945/1983 of 22nd June, defining offences and penalties in the field of consumer protection and in the agro-food industry.

a) Consumer health and safety

6.   Work on the Spanish Codex Alimentarius made considerable progress with the coming into force of technical and health regulations covering the following goods and services:

-- Edible vegetable oils;
-- Coffee;
-- Juices from fruits and other vegetables and derivatives;
-- Ice cream;
-- Table olives;
-- Tea;
-- Salt and brines;
-- Fried foods;
-- Game;
-- Detergents;
-- Communal dining rooms;
-- Food additives;
-- Vegetable preparations for infusions.

7.   The following Quality Norms were also adopted for the domestic market:

-- Curds;
-- Cooked ham, shoulder and lean pork;
-- Potatoes for consumption;
-- Cream of milk;
-- Honey;
-- Pasturised milk;
-- Sterilised milk;
-- UHT milk;
-- Evaporated milk;
-- Condensed milk;
-- Fresh peppers;
-- Cherries;
-- Dried vegetables;
-- Cultured mushrooms;
-- Fresh tomatoes.

8.   Other provisions which came into force in 1983:

-- The introduction of the prohibition of the use of boric acids for conserving crustaceans (Resolution of 27th December 1983).

-- Prohibition of the use of certain additives in bread and special breads (Resolution of 3rd January 1983).

-- Resolution of 11th April 1983 allocating an identification number (EEC) to food additives permitted for use in the preparation of foodstuffs.

-- Royal Decree 1351/1983 prohibiting the use of asbestos in the preparation and processing of foodstuffs.

-- Ministerial Order of 28th October 1983 adopting rules on the identification and purity of anti-oxidant additives used in foods.

Lists have also been published of food additives used in the following products:

-- Beer;
-- Fruit juices;
-- Edible vegetable oils;
-- Turron and marzipan cakes;
-- Table olives;
-- Aromatic agents and refreshing drinks;
-- Sweets, confectionary and liquorice products;

-- Royal Decree 2296/1983 on school vehicles;

-- Royal Decree 2505/1983, adopting regulations on the handling of foodstuffs;

-- Ministerial Order of 21st June 1983 on the characteristics and format of packaging for vegetable conserves, vegetable juices and derivatives and prepared sterilised dishes;

-- Ministerial Order of 27th July 1983, defining official methods of micro-biological analysis of drinking water intended for public consumption;

-- Royal Decree 2575/1983 on the construction characteristics of collective transport vehicles;

-- Ministerial Order of 26th October 1983 on the control and health registration of certain products (cosmetic, pharmaceutical and dietary products) and regulating advertising for them;

-- Resolution of 18th October 1983 reducing the maximum acceptable concentration of lead acetate in hair dyes.

-- Royal Decree 2814/1983 forbidding the use of recuperated regenerated polymeric materials where they come into contact with foodstuffs.

Surveillance activities:

9.   Concerning inspection, 950 reports have been made at central level and 68 548 at peripheral level, involving precautionary seizure of some goods. As a result of inspection and control activities, offences have been punished in accordance with consumer legislation: fines of Ptas 226 342 000 have been imposed at central level and Ptas 271 212 589 at peripheral level. In 451 cases details of penalties have been published in the Official Gazette: 403 of these referred to food industries and 48 to the service sector.

10.   The following activities in this area must also be emphasized:

-- The application of 35 circulars on the inspection of foodstuffs, industrial products and services, providing for surveillance of those most widely consumed or used;

-- Completion of 2 128 checks on advertising;

-- Completion of 422 checks on special products;

-- Completion of 819 checks and inspections of fats and denaturalised products;

-- 758 cases have also been completed relating to the co-ordination, investigation and inspection of complaints by international consumer organisations;

-- Complaints have been received in regard to about 30 products, of which 10 have been found in Spain and impounded. In all cases the competent bodies have been alerted so as to avoid any risk to consumers;

-- Introduction of "Inspection Days for Foodstuffs".

11.   Finally, the implementation of the Programme of Selection and Revision of Medicaments (PROSEREME) must be emphasized, which, in its first phase, resulted in the withdrawal of 111 patent medicines from the market.

Research projects:

12.   Studies and research were carried out in 1983 on the following:

-- The pattern of consumption in Spain;

-- Consumer behaviour: a theoretical approach with empirical studies;

-- The subject of consumerism in schools: analysis of textbooks in primary education;

-- Basic surveys of consumer protection;

-- The supply of consumer goods and services in Spain: special consideration of economic concentration;

-- Analysis of the creation of needs by advertising: an empirical study of the Spanish situation;

-- Applied analysis of the supply and demand of public and collective services in the urban district of Madrid;

-- The pricing of foodstuffs in Spain;

-- Consumer associations and the neighbourhood movement;

-- Consumer education in school;

-- The toy guide;

-- 11 monographs on foodstuffs.

13.   The following studies and research were also carried out as part of the Food Security Programme:

-- Five new methods of analysis;

-- Three studies on the addition of foreign fats to cocoa;

-- Research on fraudulent mixtures of oil;

-- Research into techniques involving microbes;

-- Research on new non-permitted additives;

-- Research on small concentrations of elements in foodstuffs.

Product analysis:

14.   In 1983 the Directorate General for Quality Surveillance and Analysis carried out the following analyses for human use and consumption:

-- 12 751 tests on foodstuffs and drinks;

-- 113 tests on textiles;

-- 244 tests on school material;

-- 27 tests on consumer durables.

15.   It is interesting to point out that mobile laboratories belonging to this Directorate General are stationed in twelve towns.

b) Protection of the economic interests of consumers

16.   In addition to Royal Decree 1945/1983 mentioned above, on offences and penalties and technical and health regulations which stipulate practical measures for the distribution, circulation and marketing of products, the following must also be taken into account:

-- Royal Decree 2332/1983 regulating the sale, distribution and public display of audio-visual material;

-- Royal Decree 2288/1983 establishing the special mention "Recommended by its quality" for hotels;

-- Royal Decree 2506/1983, adopting general rules for the control of the effective content of packaged foodstuffs.

2. Consumer Information

a) Labelling

17.   In the Annual Report on Developments in Spain in 1982, reference was made to Royal Decree 2058/1982 adopting the general rules for the labelling, presentation and advertising of foodstuffs. These general rules partly come into force during March 1984 and the remainder will apply from September

1984; until then certain provisions of the general rules on labelling and advertising of 1975 will continue to apply.

b) Comparative tests

18.   Royal Decree 1945/1983 on offences and penalties, already mentioned, sets out rules for carrying out analyses and publicising the results via the media.

19.   In collaboration with the Spanish Television Authority, five comparative tests have been carried out on foodstuffs and cosmetics.

c) Consultation and assistance services

20.   The Instituto Nacional del Consumo has a "consumer telephone" which gives consumer advice and deals with calls for help. In 1983 4 193 telephone calls were received: 23 per cent referring to foodstuffs, 23 per cent to advice on housing, 17 per cent regarding household costs and the remainder consisting of requests for advice on transport and communications, medicine and health, leisure and tourism, etc. This data does not include advice sought from the local Consumer Information Offices.

d) The media

21.   In addition to the customary consumer pages in the press and consumer programmes on radio and television, which in 1983 enjoyed a considerable increase in audience figures, the appearance of the bulletin "Informacion del consumo", published by the Instituto Nacional del Consumo, must be mentioned. Six issues appeared in 1983 and at the beginning of 1984 about 19 000 free copies were distributed.

e) Other information activities

22.   In 1983, a "Centre for Information and Documentation on Consumerism" (CIDOC) was created within the Instituto Nacional del Consumo. It is responsible for providing all necessary information on consumer matters to the local Consumer Information Offices, consumer organisations and the general public. The Centre has a library which consumers may consult free of charge.

23.   In 1983, some three million copies of publications were issued by the Instituto Nacional del Consumo for distribution to consumers (books, brochures, etc.).

3. Consumer education

24.   Concerning the education of children, experiments undertaken in recent years with a view to introducing consumerism as a supplementary subject in primary schools have continued to have positive results. In 1983 consumerism classes were organised in schools in the Basque country, Catalonia, Valencia and Cantabria, and the first steps in this direction have also been taken in schools in Andalucia and Madrid.

25.   Regarding consumer education for adults, reference must be made to the collaboration programmes between the Instituto Nacional del Consumo and several universities. In 1983 a Seminar took place on "The Rights of Consumers in Europe and Spain" at the University of Santander (Cantabria).

4. Redress and complaints facilities

26.   The Instituto Nacional del Consumo has a complaints service which acts as mediator between consumers and firms. In 1983, 900 complaints were lodged and 60 per cent were resolved favourably while the remainder were either passed on to other Government bodies, or no agreement was reached. The majority of complaints referred to household electrical goods, car repair workshops, dry cleaners and dyers, and house maintenance and repairs.

27.   For its part, the Directorate General for Consumer Goods Inspection received and investigated 324 complaints referring to market discipline.

III. RELATIONS BETWEEN CONSUMER POLICY AND OTHER ASPECTS OF GOVERNMENT POLICY

28.   Emphasis must be given to the favourable evolution in the trend of consumer prices which rose 12.2 per cent in 1983. This tallies with the initial forecast of the Government for whom continued inflation has been a priority area for general economic policy. This has been possible thanks to the strict monetary and fiscal policies adopted during the year, and to wage controls.

Annex

BUDGET APPROPRIATIONS FOR CONSUMER AFFAIRS (In Pesetas)

General Secretariat for Consumer Affairs	1983	1982	% Increase 1983 compared to 1982
-- Purchase of ready goods and services	386 639 000	347 566 000	11.2
-- Current transfers (grants to the Instituto Nacional del Consumo)	312 608 000	239 678 000	30.4
-- Investments	191 000 000	36 000 000	530.5
TOTAL	890 247 000	623 244 000	

The above items include the following:

-- Government grants to consumer Organisations (via the Instituto Nacional del Consumo)	146 896 000	96 896 000	51.6
-- Government grants to municipalities	120 000 000	80 000 000	50.0

I. INSTITUTIONAL DEVELOPMENTS IN THE FIELD OF CONSUMER POLICY

1.   At the beginning of the year, consumer matters at the ministerial level were moved to the Ministry of Finance from the Ministry of Commerce, which at that time ceased to exist.

2.   The government has proposed that the regional organisation for consumer matters within the County Administration be abandoned, as a result of which consumer policy resources will be concentrated in the central (governmental) and local (municipal) administrations.

3.   On the local level, 207 of the 284 municipalities -- corresponding to about 90 per cent of the population -- now have consumer advice services (October 1983).

4.   A Government Commission has been appointed with the task of carrying out a general review of consumer policy. The prevailing directives for work in this area date from 1972. It has been considered necessary now to review them in the light of subsequent experiences and with regard to the overall changes in the consumers' situation. The Commission shall examine, inter alia, the changes in private economies and the impact on consumers of new technologies. Further efforts will be made to reach more consumers in need of assistance, with the aid of and in co-operation with private organisations such as the Consumer Co-operative Movement and trade unions. The Commission will present its results in the spring of 1985.

5.   The total budget allocation for consumer issues on the national level amounts to approximately 52 million SEK, which is about the same amount as for the previous fiscal year.

II. REGULATORY OR OTHER ACTION CONCERNING CONSUMER PROTECTION, INFORMATION AND EDUCATION, AND MEANS OF REDRESS

1. Consumer protection

a) Physical protection (product safety)

6.   Guidelines for the information to be provided in the marketing of

electrical appliances have been issued by the National Board for Consumer Policies. They state inter alia that certain devices may not be installed by others than those formally competent to do so. The Board will shortly issue guidelines on the flammability of upholstered furniture and on textiles for clothing.

7.   The recording of data on accidents has continued in two more counties. In all, the records now cover some 4 000 accidents. Even at this early stage, some general conclusions can be drawn. For instance, on an annual basis, 10 per cent of the population can be expected to be involved in accidents severe enough to merit recording. The distribution indicates that about 75 per cent of the accidents are occurring in the home, in school or in leisure time, some 5 per cent are attributable to traffic and less than 20 per cent occur in industry. The statistics also show that children are involved in accidents at an increasing extent as they grow up with a peak at around 15 years. Accidents at that age are particularly common in sports and athletics.

8.   The Market Court has issued a sales ban on a toy (the Magic Egg). The toy consists of a plastic egg, with the dimensions of 4.5 x 3 centimeters, which can easily be opened. Inside the egg there is a little form modelled as an animal or an other object. When the form is put into water it grows to 20 times its size in 3 hours and to 130 times in 24 hours. The form inside the egg is similar to different kinds of gum-drops. For that reason, there is a risk that small children may swallow the form, which can enlarge inside the body and cause serious injury. The small form does not meet the requirements of the Swedish standard SS 87 00 01.

9.   A Government Commission has presented the results of a review of the Swedish system of voluntary guidelines as part of the Marketing Act system. In general, the Commission found that the system works well. Thus, adherence to the guidelines has been found to be satisfactory, or at least as satisfactory as would a system with formally binding provisions. Certain improvements have been suggested, among them greater reliance on self-regulation within industry. It is also suggested that injunctions against the sale of dangerous goods should be possible not only against retailers -- as is the case today -- but against producers and distributors as well.

b) Protection of the Consumers' economic interest

10.   The Government has introduced a Bill in Parliament suggesting an Act on Contract Terms between enterprises to be enforced on 1st July 1984. The new Act enables the Market Court to ban unfair contract terms. The Court will pay particular interest to the need to protect a party that is in a weak position. It is also made clear that the main object of the Act is to strengthen the position of smaller enterprises. Cases may be brought to Court by a union of enterprises or by the injured party to a contract.

11.   The Parliament has passed an Act on Real Estate Agents, which will come into force on 1st July 1984. Under the Act, all agents must be registered at the County Administration. To be registered, an agent must have insurance covering his commitments to sellers and buyers, a satisfactory education and be considered fit for the trade. The Act further contains provisions regarding, e.g. the advice and information that the real estate agent must give to buyers and sellers -- for instance about the conditions of the estate

and of the estimated cost of living there. The agent can be made financially responsible for losses caused by not abiding to the Act.

12.   The National Board of Consumer Policies has devoted some substantial resources to negotiating standard contracts under the provisions in the Act on Unfair Contract Terms. Apart from results achieved with single enterprises, the objective has been to reach broad arrangements covering different sectors of industry, e.g. regarding apartment rental contracts and contracts for the sale of private houses.

13.   An agreement has been reached concerning a Nordic Anti-Corrosion Code for passenger cars containing a 3-year guarantee for surface corrosion paint-damage and a 6-year guarantee for perforation and other cases of serious rust.

14.   Other agreements cover the rental of cars, guarantees for motorcycles, the rental of colour television sets and of videotape recorders, boat agent contracts and contracts for winter storage of boats.

15.   The Market Court has dealt with 13 cases brought to it by the Consumer Ombudsman. One of them concerned the aforementioned plastic egg. Another concerned the sale of furniture where a retailer, who was declared bankrupt during several months, advertised the selling out of their bankrupt stock, thereby giving a false impression of low prices. The marketing of subscriptions to magazines and membership in book clubs etc. has also been the subject of a prohibition, the issue being that consumers could discern only with difficulty their main obligation following the generous offer of e.g. a free first delivery.

SWITZERLAND

I. INSTITUTIONAL DEVELOPMENTS IN THE FIELD OF CONSUMER POLICY

1.   In accordance with the consumer protection provisions of the Constitution which were approved by referendum in 1981, the Confederation is required to take consumer protection measures while at the same time protecting national economic interests in general and respecting the principle of the freedom of trade and industry.

2.   The Federal Consumer Commission has now completed its task of preparing draft implementing legislation in two parts. The first concerns consumer information and the second makes a small number of amendments in favour of the consumer to contract and competition law.

3.   The Consumer Information Bill will prohibit the supply of certain goods and services unless they bear certain specified information. The bill also contains provisions relating to support by the Confederation for information activities of consumer organisations.

4.   The amendments to contract law and competition law aim at strengthening the consumer's position in the market, notably through a right of revocation applicable to contracts concluded in non-business premises, or made in the street, at home, in connection with advertising campaigns etc. The burden of proof is reversed as regards advertising. In 1984 it is intended to submit further consumer protection measures to the Cantons and to other interested parties.

5.   The two central consumer organisations are continuing to share a yearly grant of SF 121 500. The Consumer Information Bill should result in an increase in Federal aid.

134

II. STATUTORY AND OTHER PROVISIONS RELATING TO CONSUMER PROTECTION, INFORMATION AND EDUCATION, AND AVAILABLE REMEDIES

1. Consumer Protection

a) Health and safety (product safety)

6.   A new Order on the trading of toxic products came into force on 1st December 1983, replacing both the 1972 Order and the existing Act on the trading of toxic products. The experience of recent years in the practical application of controls over toxic products has revealed further aspects of health and commercial policy requiring modification.

7.   The Swiss Doctors' Federation and the Chemical Industries Association have created a centre to deal with the side-effects of medicines. It was confirmed that despite in-depth clinical testing, some medicines are being marketed which cause serious side-effects later on. The new centre collects information of this sort and acts as an information and advice centre between the doctors and the medicine manufacturers. Its suggestions can be reflected in the explanatory leaflets which accompany medicines. However, no direct advice is given to the public.

b) Protection of the economic interests of consumers

8.   The current Federal Act on Unfair Competition is to be replaced. A parliamentary commission has already begun discussions. The revision includes the following main points: a clearer statement of the objective (protection of good faith); restriction of the practice of inducement prices; new regulation of clearance sales and winding-up sales; and the extension of the concept of "unfairness" to unusual offers or sales practices and to general terms and conditions.

9.   By referendum in 1982, the people and the Cantons voted in favour of permanent price surveillance. Article 31(7) of the Constitution states: "To prevent abuse in price formation, the Confederation shall enact provisions concerning surveillance of prices and recommended prices applicable to goods and services offered by firms and organisations which occupy a dominant position on the market, notably by cartels and similar organisations in public or private law. Where necessary in order to achieve the desired objective these prices may be reduced." Legislation to give effect to this provision is currently being prepared.

10.   A new Consumer Credit Act is now before Parliament. This will allow better control of matters relating to small loans and hire purchase, and will to a large extent eliminate damaging social effects.

It will prove difficult for Parliament to give this Act its definitive form. The problem lies in the delicate balance to be found between the contractual freedom of the individual and adequate protection of society.

11.   A people's initiative signed by 113 000 citizens proposed the strengthening of measures to guarantee the supply of essential goods to the

population and to stop the decline of the small trader. The proposal did not receive governmental or parliamentary support. The proposed measures were considered ineffective or disproportionate. The existing Acts on unfair competition, on planning and development and on cartels were considered adequate and the initiative was withdrawn.

12.   The Act on cartels and similar organisations is to be revised. The parliamentary commissions have begun discussions. The bill includes, amongst others, a provision conferring upon consumer organisations the right to take legal action against the abuse of economic concentration on the market. The adoption of this provision remains at the discussion stage.

13.   A draft bill, completely revising the Act on Foodstuffs has been submitted for consultation to the Cantons and to other interested parties. This revision has become necessary because of certain material and organisational loopholes in the Act currently in force. The need to revise the Act became even more obvious in connection with the well-known "hormone affair". Meat and other foodstuffs will now be treated in a uniform manner. One of the important new features for the consumer is the legal competence given to the authorities to set minimum requirements for foodstuffs including meat and meat products. The scope of application will be extended to include the manufacturing stage.

14.   A new version of the Meat Control Order also reached the consultation stage. This project seeks harmonization with the provisions concerning other food products. It contains minimum requirements concerning quality, ingredients and additives as well as residues in meat. Moreover, the project also envisages a certain liberalisation of manufacturing formulae, in that the consumer is informed of the ingredients either by a specific and clear appellation in a detailed statement of the composition.

2. Consumer information

a) Labelling

15.   In accordance with a 1978 Order, retail and unit prices must be marked for sale purposes. The prices must be clearly visible and easy to read, so that the consumer is not obliged to ask the price. This applies especially to window displays. Because of the risk of break-in and theft, representatives of the jewellery and precious metals trade and the furs and antiques business have requested a modification of these regulations. However, both the consumers and the responsible authorities refuse to ease the price marking obligation.

16.   The information leaflets which accompany medicines must be more easily comprehensible to the layman. On a trial basis genuine medical information may in future be transmitted separate from the packaging. The test will show whether the system of separate information for patient and doctor will bridge the gaps in the current information leaflet system.

17.   Marking of textile products, organised on a private basis, has been used in Switzerland for 20 years. New symbols for washing and tumbler-drying have to be introduced.

b) Comparative tests

18.   Comparative tests are an important function of consumer organisations and up to thirty are carried out each year. There is international co-operation in this field.

c) Advisory services

19.   In Switzerland, government departments do not maintain consumer information centres at national or local level. However, there is indirect State approval and encouragement for private work, notably via grants and the provision of premises. Private consumer associations are thus responsible for consumer aid and information. They employ experienced staff including one or more persons responsible for giving advice.

d) Mass media

20.   An experiment with local radio will be run until 1988. Since November 1983, 36 stations have been authorised to transmit and several are already on the air. Advertising for limited times and subjects is permitted. The majority of stations also broadcast consumer information (shopping and household advice).

21.   The introduction and utilisation of a videotex interactive information system is under way. During the first Swiss videotex congress, in September 1983, the PTT carried out extended trials. Adaptation to the 335 new standardized signals, the standard of the European Conference of Postal Telecommunications Administrations, is currently being completed. A decision on the definitive introduction of videotex has not yet been taken.

3. Consumer education

22.   Efforts to introduce an Act on the prevention of disease have been abandoned. The report of the ad hoc working group met with virtually no approval from the Cantons and other parties involved, who saw it as a restriction of individual freedom and found it too expensive. The proposal was to raise taxes on alcohol, limit tobacco advertising even further and extend the Act on Foodstuffs.

23.   Primary education is the responsibility of the Cantons and control in this area is therefore decentralised. Several Cantons, teachers and consumer and economic organisations are encouraging consumer education. Classes in the domestic sciences, the mainstay of consumer education, are offered more frequently, for boys as well as for girls.

4. Remedies and complaints procedures

24.   The Cantons are currently in the process of establishing a quick and simple legal procedure for disputes involving amounts not exceeding SF 8 000 arising from contracts concluded between end consumers and suppliers. This is based on a provision of the Constitution and on the Order fixing monetary

limits in procedures concerning consumer protection, which came into force in 1982.

25.   80 per cent of all direct selling houses are members of an association which undertakes to respect a code of conduct. There is a complaints body with parity representation and a five day cooling-off period for all sales contracts and orders.

III. RELATIONSHIP BETWEEN CONSUMER POLICY AND OTHER ASPECTS OF GOVERNMENTAL POLICY

26.   Inflation almost halved in 1983, falling from a yearly average of 5.7 per cent to 2.9 per cent, its lowest level since 1978 (1 per cent).

27.   Parliament adopted an Act on the Protection of the Environment. The Act aims to protect mankind, animals and plants and their interrelations and habitat from damage or interference, and to preserve soil fertility. It also includes provisions to encourage environmental protection activities. After long discussion the right to take legal action has been granted to environmental protection organisations.

28.   A referendum rejected an Article of the Constitution on energy. The proposal was considered too centralised and too restrictive of economic freedom. New ways of encouraging the rational use of energy are now being sought; measures are also necessary to counteract the decline of forests. The future Act on Consumer Information will make it possible to introduce compulsory energy labelling.